On FIRE:

A Concise Account of
Acts and Messages
of the Holy Spirit
that will

Ignite Your Faith

On FIRE:

A Concise Account of Acts and Messages of the Holy Spirit that will

Ignite Your Faith

Dr. Sammy O. Joseph

Pulse Publishing House

© 2017 Sammy O. Joseph

Published in the United Kingdom by
Pulse Publishing House
Box 15129
Birmingham
England
B45 5DJ
pulsepublishinghouse@harvestways.org

All rights reserved. No part of this publication may be reproduced, stored in a retrieval system, or be transmitted, in any form, or by any means, mechanical, electronic, photocopying or otherwise without prior written consent of the publisher.

Bible quotes are from the King James Version of the Bible unless otherwise stated.

Amplified quotes are from the Amplified Bible, © copyright 1995 by The Zondervan Corporation and The Lockman Foundation.

Cover design and typesetting by Pulse Publishing House, England.

Printed in England.

ISBN 978-0-9567298-5-9

Contents

Acknowledgement — *vii*

Dedication — *ix*

1 *The Build Up* — *1*

2 *Faith for Cartoons* — *9*

3 *Rekindled Fire* — *21*

4 *Crockery Pot on Fire* — *43*

5 *Live on Fire: I've Never Done this Before* — *59*

6 *Fire at Harrow* — *91*

7 *Stoked* — *137*

8 *Never Say: I Ain't Got Nothin'* — *153*

Epilog — *183*

Acknowledgement

From the very depth of my heart, I thankfully and gratefully acknowledge my friend Dr. Alden Taylor and his beautiful wife, Dr. Katarina Taylor for birthing this book without even realizing it. They couldn't ever have suspected their pivotal roles in the birthing process: That alone explains the reason for this formal acknowledgement of their combo-seed of genuine friendship, openness and covenant partnership in the Gospel!

When in summer 2014 we had met in Pensacola, Florida; little had any of us known what pleasant odors, our different giftings would release into the *potpourri pot* of friendship! However as we began to communicate what great things we could together accomplish for the Lord of Hosts, it became clearer we could team up — and by so doing become stronger in accomplishing our assignments and pursuits.

Whenever God had wanted to accomplish a task on earth, He had always used — and still does use humans to further His counsel. Thus, I am eternally grateful to God for the doors He had this wonderful couple open to us during the very first *International Experience Harvestways Conference*, anywhere in the world! The warmth, humility, love, deep intellectual — and personal vulnerabilities we shared together had formed the seal of our bonds in friendship! We have from that evolved to become friends on a mission, as ministers of His grace! For this reason, I celebrate you, both.

Dedication

As is my custom, I dedicate this piece of work to the two very beautiful young ladies and three handsome gentlemen I am so privileged to — with every ounce of godly pride — call my children: Gabby, David, Daniel, Prissy 'Co-co' — and our dear Apostle, Paul. THANK YOU all so very much, for your exceptional encouragement and release of me to perform the ministry of the Lord, to which I had been called!

I honor you, deeply — and do love you!

■ CHAPTER ONE

The Build Up

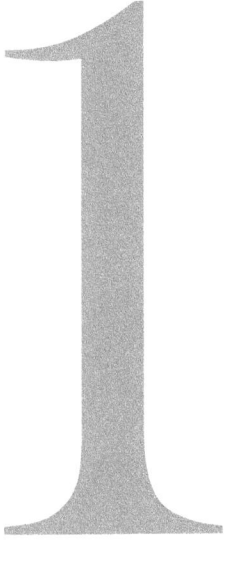

1
The Build Up

November 8, 2014 had been a memorable day: It had been the very first day of a *HarvestWays Conference* anywhere in the world!

That conference had been a local event. Fairly publicized in the local suburb of Northfield — our *Jerusalem*. Because we'd rented from a local association, we had not been allowed to display banners or posters outside the hall — as always had been the culture in the United Kingdom for time immemorial! You could erect banners or billboards on public lands *only* with an approval from the City Council of your jurisdiction; you may not even be permitted placing ordinary posters on property-walls if you weren't the outright registered owner!

That night, twenty-two souls had gathered — taking into magnanimous consideration, three pastor-friends who had turned up to honor our invitation. (*When last had we welcomed such a 'crowd'?*) We had been overwhelmed with joy. As we had proceeded worshipping the Lord, the Holy Spirit had clearly spoken:

> *"I AM going to take this (Experience Harvestways) conference internationally. I will readily back it up with great outpouring of grace and virtue; signs and wonders!"*

We had all rejoiced, exceedingly *in* faith!

Every January ...

At *Sammy Joseph Ministries*, every January is designated unto the Lord in corporate fasting and prayer! January 2015 was no different. We had prayed, praised — and called upon the name of the Lord of hosts over the many issues that defiantly stared us in the eyes! We had bathed the ministries, our church families and all, in prayer. Then the Lord had added specific direction unto us: *"Set your eyes towards the West: Canada and the United States ..."* These would become our beachhead for the international edition of the conference!

Now, I had been to Canada previously in 2013 on a familiarization visit. It had *not* looked a ripe, open door at the time for the move God had in mind *through* us. So we'd merely waited on Him — whilst we had focused our minds on other ministerial matters. Unbeknown to me, Dr. Alden and Dr. Katarina (Kat) Taylor had been specifically instructed of the Lord to host our first international conference. As always is my tradition, I would place a New Year's call — that contained prayers and a short summary of the word of the Lord to me about the particular year — to a crop of names on my list, region by region; continent by continent. It had been Canada's turn; I had the Taylors — and boom, the ignition switch had been turned on! As we had neared the end of our conversation and had prayed that New Year's day, they had openly confirmed their express willingness to spearhead the thrust of the very first *'International Experience Harvestways Conference 2015'*. They had also extended our name to vital connections in the United States of America. *Thus had begun the commencement of the fulfilment of the word of the Lord to us November 8, 2014.*

I had ministered over the radio and television in America — even to a worldwide live audience of over 100 million souls. Doors of ministry had opened to churches both in Ontario, Canada — and Michigan, USA.

This project in your hand contains the true, live-accounts of the visitations of the Holy Spirit among His people as I had ventured out in faith to do the Lord's bidding. God had me prepared, willing hearts. After this North American debut in 2015, the Holy Spirit had taken same *International Experience Harvestways* conference to Kenya, April / May 2016. There in East Africa, God had performed every word spoken through this very tongue of mine. One of the Bishops in the world's greatest rift valley settlement — the Nakuru Rift Valley — Bishop Joseph Madadi had been so touched that he had pre-booked me as one of the keynote speakers at their world conference in 2017, that would involve over 200 pastors and bishops from four or five countries from the East and Southern African region.

'Who alone is sufficient for these things?' as Apostle Paul had asked the Corinthians? Only that God to Whom be all the praise for unending years to come is! And as He gives me the grace, I shall continue to engage in taking the most meaningful risks that will continue to bear Heaven — and I — more than equitable rewards!

These following pages therefore contain summary

accounts of events — and few original sermon outlines at the maiden *International Experience Harvestways Conference* USA and Canada, 2015. (Where necessary, real names have been changed to protect identities).

Chapter Two
Faith for Cartoons

2

Faith for Cartoons

It had been a drizzly, early spring evening in the Motown city. I had flown eight hours — and eventually arrived Tecumseh, Ontario via the Dwayne International Airport, Detroit, USA. This would be a ten-day mission; one that I would never forget: Busy and fulfilling. Dr. Alden had met me at *DTW*; hugged and slung my backpack on one of his shoulders. He had also wanted to wheel my baggage but I hadn't let him, out of sheer respect. He and his wife Kat had drawn out the details of my itinerary. By the looks of it, there wouldn't be one lazy time! Their chart had ranged from un-documented one-on-one visitations at the hospitals to all I had explained in *Chapter 1*.

By April 10 between the three of us, we had indeed had a reward for our labor! Our Heavenly Father had rewarded us with jaw-dropping miracles. Let's start with Miela, shall we?

Miela

Miela (not her real name) was of mixed roots: A Native mother (Truisa, not her real name) and an African-American father from Detroit city. Methinks it's much easier for a few brothers to just go "sub" through the Detroit–Windsor tunnel or saunter across the Ambassador Bridge mainly to find love in Canada. Reciprocally too, some females in Canada have this rare, spontaneous affinity with their male counterparts across the river! Also, Canada operated that special blend of colonial British *welfarist* and the American *capitalist* economies: No one would seek to put behind bars for non-payment of child support, an American absentee father who had happily sown his wild oats in the land of the Cannucks! So, in a way, it's a "win-win" for either side, as they think!

Anyway, Miela was a gorgeous-looking seventeen year-old young lady. She and her boyfriend had partied *hard* that weekend. She had ended up getting drunk — and high, on some dry narcotics! Her consciousness had quickly faded away! Into the second day of an

ER admission, she hadn't regained consciousness. When we had alighted upon her floor in the intensive care unit (ICU) of the Windsor Regional Hospital — Metropolitan Campus, we had found her in her third day: Her state of stupor had resulted from high and dangerous levels of intoxication and poisoning. Hospital authorities had had her heavily sedated. Her eye-lids had been glued–up (as it were), by a thick, brown wax!

I had gazed at the intravenous drip supply in one of her arms — and the two tubes that had been inserted into her mouth. My heart must have skipped a heartbeat or two. A quick glance at the blood pressure monitor that had beeped periodically at the height of her bed had registered in red *LED* lights, an astonishing *173/108* reading! That, by every means was high, for a teenager. Only occasional gasps for breath had convinced me she hadn't gained the confidence of the shroud!

Truisa and her fifteen year old son had kept vigil at Miela's bedside, in turns. The skins on their foreheads had been wrinkly — and their teary eyes; very heavy, drowsy from sleep and rest deprivation, combined! Their fears had *not* been unfounded: Anyone could tell that the spirit of death had hoovered like a vulture over that room. But my friend and I had visited here in the *bona fide* authority of the Great Physician! We would address the ominous, black, gloomy clouds to billow away — and the joy of the Lord to take its place!

I had had my right hand laid on the pastor's back as he had prayed for Miela. She hadn't produced *any* muscular movement apart from the short gasps for breath drawn from her oxygen face-mask!

After Dr. Taylor had prayed, the Lord had given me a flashing vision: I had seen Miela arise from that same bed — and taken two strong steps in total health — before bursting into a run! Oh, by the gift of interpretation of dreams and visions, I knew the symbolism of that vision; so I had prophesied accordingly, by the same Holy Spirit:

> *"You will be discharged from this same hospital bed this very weekend — in mere two days from today!"*

All other pairs of eyes in that room had turned on me in that kind of inquisitive; "Are-you-sure?" looks. Even I had been dazed by those words that had tumbled out of *my* mouth. But I hadn't *meant* to utter them; I must have been *drunk*, too. (But I couldn't have apologized for having being drunk with the right kind of wine — the Holy Spirit. Or could I?) The release of those words had had my faith run amuck! I could feel the glow of a heat, all over me. I had confessed the same to everyone in that hospital room that mid-afternoon. My palms had become red and moist as I had announced with repeated, assured nods of the head:

> "You watch; she'd be perfectly alright by this weekend just as the Lord has said!"

Operating in my office as a prophet — God's spokesperson declaring His mindset — ever always gladdens my spirit. But doing the work of an evangelist in any capacity yields me even greater joy. So I had doubled on my dose of rejoicing: Approached Miela's younger brother with a quick presentation of Christ's message.

The young man's neckline had been heavily-bedecked in thick, golden bling. Six of his ten fingers also had big beautiful rings on; I'd had to cast a quick second look to be sure of what my eyes had seen! He had flashed me a smile that had a false golden incisor. *('What had I gotten myself into, now?')* He'd completed his *catchy* outlook with a baseball cap and a black leather jacket. His hip-pop gear had definitely been overtly in tone — and my spirit had picked on the emptiness of his soul! He had looked 'really super cool' and *very* complete but my spirit had realized he had lacked something precious: Peace of mind! Presenting and offering to humans the Prince of Peace in a simple understandable way remains the primary, sole hallmark of an evangelist!

I hadn't beaten around the bush. I had hit *very* fast where it hurts, *intentionally!* And thank goodness, it *had* paid off. (It always does!)

In no time, the extravagant youth had asked the LORD, Jesus Christ to come into his young heart. I'd turned to my accomplice-in-crime and asked him to lead the youth to Christ, being my original lead to this family. Dr. Taylor had prayed — and had also encouraged him to join their local church assembly to undergo his discipleship classes in order to grow in his new-found faith in Christ. The tormented mom and teenaged son had been so grateful! We had exchanged pleasantries and well-wishes as we parted!

We had not driven half an hour when the pastor's phone had rung. He had burst out laughing, hysterically. I had looked into his eyes, confused, as I had strained to eavesdrop on the conversation but I couldn't hear anything! Both the car's engine and the high-pitched female voice at the other end hadn't oscillated well with me! So I had been forced to inquire: *"What's going on, sir?"* I think I had demanded, a little forcefully, but I had been responded to with the reply: *"You have to have the phone ..."*

My friend had handed me his cell phone. However, he had kept laughing uncontrollably, still. The car cabin had felt like having gained a few degrees in temperature: You could literally feel it. At the first instinct, I had thought it had been Dr. Kat on the phone. I had thought they both, on intent, were playing a game of mischief on me. (Both could be mischievous sometimes — particularly if you were at the center of their bewilderment-moments!) But I had been wrong; the caller had corrected me: *"I am Neeta"*.

"Neeta? Neeta?? Neeta???" I had engaged my thought process in quick-mode. *"Emm ... pardon me, Neeta; I wouldn't know of anyone called Neeta! Please could you tell me where we'd last met?"*

Within a second, my mind had paced a thousand thoughts — and a thousand-and-one-cities. Yet, there had been no slightest clue of who Neeta was!

Dr. Taylor had tried hard to concentrate on his driving. Neeta too had burst out laughing. Amidst the ensuing confusion she had quickly disclosed:

"OK! You and I have never met, but I have some awesome Good news for you: I am Miela's auntie; Miela, the young intoxicated lady you and the pastor had just visited at the Met ICU!"

"And what about her?" I had inquired as I'd pressed the phone's speaker closer to my hearing! *What could so suddenly have transpired?*; I had questioned, deep within me?

"Well, Dr. Joseph, I'm here to confirm to you that Miela is awake — fully conscious; watching cartoons on the Telly!"
I had *not* concluded whether or not I'd been the object of a silly, foolish prank; after all, it had been an 'April Fool's Day'. So I had belted*: "You can't be serious; that's not true!"*

We'd traded back and forth same rhymes like kindergarten kids a few times — before she had asked me to kindly hand back the cell phone to her pastor who had in the intervening period, maintained his own sense of hysterical laughter!

Neeta had arrived at the conclusion she had needed to convince my doubting-Thomas' heart! She had summoned her pastor to pull his car over at a convenient parking space off Tecumseh Road as she and her husband would double up with us in no time!

The street sign arrowed *McDougall Avenue*. We had turned off it onto a huge *Burger King* parking lot. Soon, a white SUV had pulled up adjacent us. The string of events that had sequenced would boggle any one mind! This parking lot would become a holy ground, in no time.

This chapter has focused mainly upon Miela's 'unbelievable' miracle. It's about time we discovered what had transpired at the parking lot!

Chapter Three
Rekindled Fire

Rekindled Fire

Fires start by being kindled — and every so often require re-kindling. We re-kindle a fire whose ebbs are reducing — and tongues, shortening.

Fires can burn low due to restrictions in fuel supply. Fires can be dampened by chemical additives that are designed to extinguish them. (Fire fighters would tremendously agree with me on that point). But here is even greater news about fires: They can be restored to burn with greater passion and intensity more than as at the freshest!

Possibly your passion for a person, place or thing you once held very dearly had suffered a low-ebb; I have great news for you: You can be re-kindled, yet again!

You will know you've been rekindled *when* you begin to see the manifestation of *your* signs. The Jewish captives by the River of Babylon had wished upon themselves the quickening and unraveling of a bright new dawn foretold by Prophet Jeremiah. Their forefathers had scorned, disdained — and reduced the lonely prophet into a laughing stock. But not anymore! Not when they had become captives to the merciless Babylonians. In captivity, they had remembered his precise predictions and prophecies. In bondage, they had longed for their emancipation at the expiration of the prophetic mandate! So they had sat down to reflect — and had sung this mournful song:

> *"By the rivers of Babylon, there we sat don, yea, we wept, when we remembered Zion.*
>
> *We hanged our harps upon the willows in the midst thereof.*
>
> *For there they that carried us away captive required of us a song; and they that wasted us required of us mirth, saying, Sing us one of those songs of Zion.*
>
> *How shall we sing the LORD's song in a strange land?*

If I forge thee, O Jerusalem, let my right hand forget her cunning.

If I do not remember thee, O Jerusalem, let my tongue cleave to the roof of my mouth; if I prefer not Jerusalem above my chief joy.

Remember, O LORD, the children of Edom, in the day of Jerusalem; who said, Rase it, rase it, even to the foundation thereof.

O daughter of Babylon, who art to be destroyed; happy shall he be, that rewardeth thee as thou hast served us.

Happy shall he be, that taketh and dasheth thy little ones against the stones."
| Psalms 137: 1-9

Spiritual Milestones

In the earlier centuries up until the sixties and seventies when there were no satellite devices, the federal government erected milestones on all major highways. These on one side showed directions and mileage-readings *to* destinations on a road of travel — and on the other side — corresponding readings *from* origins of travel. Same does God.

Our God, the Ancient of days, still does highlight direction and mileage to His children's earthly sojourn in the form of tell-all spiritual milestones — no matter how small or insignificant they might seem. Never trivialize signs — much as you wouldn't trivialize the necessity of your modern-day satellite navigation / global positioning system device!

Normally, God's milestones manifest of their own accord, consistently through the route, just as in the ancient times: You would notice them, conspicuously displayed by the side of the road! In the same token, you normally wouldn't necessarily have to seek or beg God for spiritual milestones — except you're been gawky! Think about the way you gained an admission prayerfully sought for. Or had met your spouse who daily reciprocates your love! Or the inner alarms that had warned of a fraudster; or the like!

Spiritual signs however, may *not* always be pleasant! Understandably, the natural human's disposition would prefer to rather experience positive, pleasant signs that gladden their hearts rather than otherwise! Some signs however are meant to jolt us awake if we were slumbering, or point us in re-direction were we traveling on a wrong route. Some other signs would challenge us, cause us to reflect deeply, build our spirit; deepen our roots and cause us to walk on higher planes of consecration with God. These are the signs that may be implausibly desirable by our physical disposition.

Shouldn't any have rightly suspected God was setting one up for a test of higher walk much as He had Prophet Habakkuk when in spite of his having dug round and dunged the fig; fed and kept the sheep, both efforts had proved abortive?

> *"Although the fig tree shall not blossom, neither shall fruit be in the vines; the labor of the olive shall fail, and the fields shall yield no meat; the flock shall be cut off from the fold, and there shall be no herd in the stalls."*

While this is not in any way making an excuse for bad behavior or conduct, it would take a dedicated, faithful, sensitive spirit to recognize, heed a higher call — and separate away from the mundane elements of the world at such calamitous times as had been suffered by Prophet Habakkuk.

The prophet wouldn't give up on his joy; the source of his deep-rooted strength in God! He said he would rejoice even when the physical signs did *not* warrant a favorable disposition:

> *Yet will I rejoice in the LORD, I will joy in the*

God of my salvation."
| Habakkuk 3:17-18

At the Burger King Parking Lot

Right there at the *Burger King* parking lot, the God of Heaven Who is so passionate about each of us was about to initiate Mikel and his wife, Neeta into a consecrated closer walk with Himself! Miela had been prayed for barely an hour earlier — and now, she had miraculously awoken from a medically induced coma, sat up in bed and watched cartoons on the TV!

Who could do that but God Almighty!

More, Miela had been given the 'all clear' bill of health; she *would* be out of the hospital's *ICU* by the end of the week as the Holy Spirit had said! She had indeed been ready for what nurses and doctors had termed *"the miraculous discharge never witnessed in the history of the Met."* that weekend, but for a few concerns in the heart of her doubtful mom, Truisa.

Truisa had requested the authorities Miela be further held until the following Monday, April 6th. Accordingly, the staff had complied!

Monday had dawned — and Miela had been clean

and sober. Clean. Dry. Sparkling; ready to soar like the proverbial phoenix, rising from its own ashes, never again to die! Every word you read about this astounding miracle had become an official document of the Ministry of Health of Ontario province, Canada!

Behold, when you're rekindled — and on fire for God, signs will attest your every move. Even your *exhale* will condense power! However, the day your signs diminish may be the days the amber warning lights on your spirit-man's dashboard have begun to blink, warning *you* of impending great troubles! The disappearance of your sign(s) may be attributable to your making light the covenant God made with you as had Prophet Samson of old on the laps of Delilah. (Only you may tell what milepost you are at on your journey with the Lord; I may not be able to speak for you).

When however you're rekindled by the Holy Spirit, your heart will rejoice — and your mouth, laugh again. Your 'old', brittle bones will suddenly absorb strength; your face, brightened like a summer morning's dawn — and your joy will know no bounds!

When God speaks through your lips — and those words come to pass — you will know beyond every iota of disbelief that power has been switched on on the inside of you. You gain somewhat, an ounce of self-confidence. You feel a pleasant rush of anointing surge through your spirit like it does through a live circuit. Heaven's supernatural flows are visibly undeniable: Doors on heavenly-oiled hinges swing open of their own accord! Miracles daily attest everyday-existence. Life becomes enthralling to live! May you enter into *this* new realm of the overflow, today!

At the *Burger King* parking lot, this happy man — whom I estimated was in his early-fifties had jumped out of theirs and had approached my friend's car.

"I'm Mikel," I'd heard him shout as soon as his feet had hit the ground in heavy, hasted paces. He had only paused to look into my eyes to see if both had locked four! Like a bolt of lightning, he'd rounded off the rear of their van to the passenger-side of ours. I had hurriedly alighted to meet him.

"I am Sammy Joseph from Birmingham, England" I'd introduced myself without drawing a breath! Mikel's original tight-gripping handshake had progressed onto an unexpected tight, brotherly, bear hug. A spontaneous reaction from a large heart, it had happened on an hyped adrenalin surge, I suppose!

"I'm Neeta's husband: The lady you just conversed with on

the phone …" He had pointed at the occupant of the passenger seat in their van before continuing: *"We only wanted meet you face to face to let you know how grateful to God we are. We are Miela's uncle and aunt! Her drastic recovery this morning we know, is nothing short of God's supernatural act!"*

Tears had welled up in my eyes as I'd taken Mikel's hands in mine. We'd both taken a few steps towards Neeta who still had sat in their van. Some gentle breeze had washed over my skin in this spring sunshine; His unmistakable presence had been conspicuously felt. Instinctively, I knew *the* fire was on: *The fire of God's Holy Spirit!* But I would later get to learn more about Mikel and Neeta from their pastor, my friend Dr. Taylor.

Mikel, a quiet character was the exact opposite of his wife Neeta. Today's miraculously news had been a climactic catalyst to their need wanting to meet "the visiting English preacher!" Both he and his wife had dutifully patrolled church members' homes on service-days and offered them free transportation to and fro a traveling distance of almost fifty minutes.

Once the burly man showed up at your door, he entertained no excuses. He merely knocked the door; poked his head through — and motioned you out with a nod towards his van. No one ever said "No" to his visits which by now had become a routinely habit he had accustomed to with great joy. The couples' zeal as a team had swashed over me the pleasant feeling of how-wonderful-it-would-be-to-have-more-evangelist-couples-like-these-in-churches! Mikel and Neeta always possessed the inner strength to be winsome. They both are an invaluable asset to the work of the Lord! Even though of informal education, what gifts and talents they possessed had heartily been re-ploughed into the soil of human hearts they had encountered! But the wife had an unspoken need!

Now, every anointed minister of the Lord *ought to* know that instant the Holy Spirit is about to switch into action. You must *not* ignore His signs! Personally, many a time, my heart had 'leapt for joy'; its pace, quickened. Some other time, my eyes had moistened, from the welled-up overflow of compassion caused by His presence. At such times, I had realized it had been time to help someone in dire need. A few times, a sharp jolt on my body part had quickened me to someone's exact diseased part that had needed being healed. I have come to learn by faith and the gift of the word of knowledge / wisdom that I have to call out those diseases by name; rebuke and command them to leave their hosts' bodies in the worthy name of Jesus. Not a few times, my palms had become red-hot — and sweaty! You see, whenever any of these had occurred to me, I had come to learn that the Holy Spirit was about to do a spectacular work. Did He not promise in His word to put a word in season in our mouth? | Psalms 81:10. Yet on a few occasions — like today, the hairs on my body had stood erect with visible goose-pimples at their bases as if someone had affectionately touched me. Unless you cared less in your response to His affection, you *should* know when the Holy Spirit is ready to use you: Your spirit would know when the Lord's presence is nearest!

As I'm about to speak, teach or preach God's words, I dared not utter a word until I had awaited His readiness *within* me! My knees sometimes had buckled slightly — or my lips had needed moistening. Not out of fear of what to say, but rather in acknowledgement of the yielding of my vessel unto Him, to fully use. My dry lips are not always conspicuous except I called your attention to them. This is the reason I always had my bottle of water with me at the pulpit. Call me what you may; possibly a "water-bottle preacher", but I *know* my signs. I've learned my cup had to be fully washed and drained before His grace had outpoured! Sometimes I have been totally overwhelmed by sudden hot tears streaking down my cheeks whilst in the middle of a sermon. You could easily have dubbed me 'cry-baby', but that's also alright. Those tears had a reason: Set men free from everything that causes them to weep and lament! (Hardly would any believe there was a season in my life — that had stretched almost three decades — during which my tear ducts had dried up!)

What am I trying to pass across?

Whatever it takes; you must pay attention to the revealing sign(s) that the presence of the Lord is apparent to accomplish a major task through you.

My encounter with Mikel and Neeta had been very uncharacteristic. As I'd strolled towards Neeta, I'd felt *that* gentle wind-blow on my skin as I have earlier described. I had been positioned between both vehicles. I'd spoken briefly with Neeta. After all the excitement of a face-to-face meeting had somewhat cooled off, I had asked us to say a quick word of prayer holding hands in a chain! I'd closed my eyes — and opened my mouth to talk to our Heavenly Father. Suddenly, I'd become dumb: Speechless. Instinctively, I had received a word of knowledge in my spirit man. So I had stopped praying — and had asked everyone to open their eyes … That must have been a bit absurd, mustn't it? Hands still held in a chain — eyes opened, my tongue had loosed. These words had tumbled out unrestrained: *"The Lord says you're going to Niagara Falls, isn't that true?"*

I had first taken a look at the couple and quickly turned to look at my friend with that 'What's-Happening-Here?' surprise look!

I had shrugged too, but had continued: *"How could I have known that except by the Holy Spirit!"*

Friends, you too can be privy to highly sensitive, hidden mysteries in the Spirit — if you only would practice listening to His voice. The Holy Spirit has a strong sense of humor: *"You're on your way to Niagara Falls but the Lord intended you to be here at my conference!"* I had said with raised eyebrows.

"Awwwwwww; we're so sorry, Dr. Joseph. Our holiday had been pre-booked before we'd learned of your program — and we couldn't cancel it!" Neeta had said.

"So when are you returning from this planned trip?" I had probed further with a wistful grimace of an expression?

"Sunday evening," Mikel had responded!

"OK, well, umm; the Lord says you're gonna have a miracle at Niagara Falls."

"What sort of miracle?" Neeta had intuitively inquired.

Since the Lord hadn't told me specifically what miracle it was they should be expecting, even I couldn't reveal to them what had awaited them at the largest natural frontier between Canada and the United States.

So I had replied: *"I wouldn't know. The Lord didn't specifically tell me what particular miracle you were to expect — but you will remember this very day, Wednesday April 1, 2015 that the Lord said through my mouth that you're gonna have a miracle at Niagara Falls because He's sent His angels ahead of you!"*

With the burden rolled off me, now I could re-commence praying for the departing couple. I had indeed thanked the Lord for bringing us to meet face to face for this impartation. Thereafter, my friend and I had waved them *'Bye!'* Now, this kind of an impromptu encounter at an empty, open parking lot was by all means strange, to the core. But the Holy Spirit had orchestrated it. The evidence of His presence had been all too hard to deny. Towards the end of the Saturday morning service in Harrow where I had preached the most uncustomary Easter message, a text message had surfaced on Dr. Taylor's cell phone. It had been sent by Mikel and had stated that Neeta had had a serious health crisis — and had needed to dial 911! He reportedly mentioned that his wife had been in a critical condition — and had been airlifted to the *ICU* of London Hospital, Ontario,

Canada!

If you were I, would you have panicked at such information?

Neeta and Mikel are residents of Windsor. Neeta had, according to Mikel *"being pronounced dead"* at the scene at Niagara Falls by paramedics who had answered his *911* call. Unbeknown to me, Neeta had had an ongoing medical condition with her liver and bowels. She had often also suffered seizures. Doctors in Windsor had been unable to properly diagnose the cause; neither had they enough funding to transfer her case onto specialists in more technically advanced city like Toronto or London. Some dialysis had been offered her in the past — but that just had been it.

Mikel had been too overwhelmed to think as the ambulance crew dispatched had readied the shroud and the stretcher! Then, suddenly, there had been a stirring of a thought within him. He had remembered *our* encounter the previous day. He then had gently laid his right hand on his wife's lifeless body and according to him: *"I had simply reminded God the words of His servant that we would experience our own miracle at Niagara Falls as God's angels had been sent ahead of us. I had whispered a quick prayer: 'Lord, please remember Your words!' "*

And He had!

Suddenly, there had been a fluttery movement underneath the shroud: Neeta had sneezed — and the ambulance crew had been shell-shocked! They had carefully unzipped the shroud, checked her pulse — and had ever so efficiently connected her onto an oxygen mask. Then quickly, onto an ambulance helicopter — and off to London Hospital, Ontario.

Those had been Mikel's exact description of account of events on that phone call to Dr. Taylor later that evening! He had asked the church for continued prayers.

When this happening had been announced at the meeting, folk had panicked. Some others had started to entreat the Lord that Neeta lives. But I had done neither; not out of pride, I actually just couldn't have done anything out of the deep conviction in my spirit. You see, I had a pre-knowledge of the exact words of prophecy God had uttered through my mouth the day prior. That knowledge had propelled my faith to shoot sky high! To have started to raise *any* intercessory — rather than thanksgiving-prayer would have been tantamount to succumbing to the spirit of unbelief! Same goes for *any* situation in which you too might find yourself: If you have located the *rhema* word for that situation, you would do well to start giving thanks to God even when the evidence proves contrary. Jesus taught us to do *just* that many a time in His teachings!

Unbelief is simply defined as believing, yet not believing. It is a robber of faith and mighty works of the Holy Spirit. Unbelief, if allowed, opens the doors unto its accomplice: Doubt. Now, you can't afford to be double-minded if you would receive the Father's promise! Apostle James says:

> *"If any of you lacks wisdom, let him ask of God, that giveth to all men liberally, and upbraideth not; and it shall be given him.*
>
> *But let him ask in faith, nothing wavering. For he that wavereth is like a wave of the sea driven with the wind and tossed.*
>
> *For let not that man think that he shall receive anything of the Lord. A double minded man is unstable in all his ways."*
>
> | James 1:5–8

If you would waver at God's promises through unbelief and doubts, you've already had your reward: *Nothing!* God says you would be unstable in all your ways!

I was not unstable in the spirit of my mind; neither was I willing to let go of Neeta's miracle through unbelief! That would have been most offensive to the Holy Spirit!

One surety any true servant of God brings with them into a territory is *not* the burden of grief, sadness and sorrow. Rather, the Bible says *we* carry a potent anointing of everlasting joy upon our heads. It also adds: We — and whoever receives our calling — shall receive joy and gladness; and sadness — and sorrow and mourning shall flee away (*Cf. Isaiah 51:11*). Notice Isaiah's phrase: *"flee away."* Why recall a being already on a flight for safety? Rather, we are to chase after — and rouse to flight, *any* spirit contrary to that of the Holy One of Israel!

I am most assuredly persuaded that I carry the unction of the Almighty God! Anywhere I am sent, I proudly thump my chest that nothing; absolutely nothing, dies near me. Nothing even falls sick near me. I always boast of the oil upon my head, that I single-handedly raised five great ministers of the Lord from infancy — and that only once did one of them ever visit the hospital throughout my parenting career!

You see, I am a carrier of the fire that drives demonic forces away. I carry the oil that overflows with joy. That oil on my head also protects and preserves the lives of all under my umbrella!

After the medical specialists had ran their various tests, it had eventually emerged that Neeta would need a new right kidney.

So God had allowed Neeta the passage crossing territories in part, in order for her to access better medical facilities that would lead to a life-saving diagnosis in London. Same treatment the authorities in Windsor had hitherto denied her! This development in itself had been a part-miracle! Though certified well — and had been discharged April 10, 2015; Neeta's prognostic specialist consultancy and further periodic checks would continue. As at the time of publishing this book, Neeta was alive and well. Though she continues her dialysis treatment, I am assured God will perfect her health — just because He had spoken it! Both Neeta and Mikel had come to that conclusion: Neeta's near-fatal experience with the chilling, cold hands of death *"had been a re-commissioning effort by the Holy Spirit to get us more committed to the work of evangelism,"* according to Mikel. Well, that's one interpretation. To me, I had thought it had been a wake-up call to the awareness of yet another milestone in their faith journeys!

I thus declare over you this day:

"You too will testify of the power of God you have experienced when the fire of the Holy Spirit kindles — or re-kindles — upon you!"

Neither Mikel nor Neeta may have been called into the five-fold ministry; the public speaking, traveling, prophetic or pastoring ministry. Everyone however had testified to the new surge of enthusiasm evident in their lives, *just* because of a renewed, re-kindled fire of God!

Chapter Four

Crockery Pot on Fire!

4

Crockery Pot on Fire!

I greatly rejoice in the faith-renewal of Neeta and Mikel as they had re-dedicated their lives to the service of the Lord through the local church. They had found a winning formula that leads to fulfilment in purposing to serve the Lord with fervor, candor and enthusiasm in their area of gifting. Possibly, that's as much as they both are called to *do* in the Kingdom! That is the real deal, right there: *Discovery*. The discovery of your niche in this vast Heavenly assignment!

We all have *a* niche to fill; a spot to dote upon, excel and shine at. Your position of service awaits your discovery: You should *never* ever want to exhaust your available energies and reserves on this side of eternity only to stand before God face to face and realize your entire livelihood had been spent on fruitless labor. Mere nothingness! The wisest man that ever lived, Solomon, refers to that kind of existential mindset as:

> *"Vapor of vapors and futilities, says the Preacher. All is futility (emptiness, falsity, vainglory, and transitoriness)!"*
> | Ecclesiastes 12:8; Amp.

No More Excuses

Are you still able to afford proffering excuses that will drift you away from Kingdom call to duty? Excuses of the like: *"I haven't got a prominent gift; that just seems to be it!"* Or *"I do work full-time; the bills won't pay themselves at the end of the month, will they?"* These are just two of the commonest misconceptions tabled by most christians who should have mattered greatly in the hands of the Lord, but have chosen to be perfect *'excusapologetics.'* (That's my word-coinage for people who are adept at proffering nothing but excuses; people who only always see the cup as half-empty rather than half-full!)

What of this other excuse: *"I am tired of this whole thing; it just doesn't seem to be going anywhere!"* This sure sounded like emanating from the lips of a spouse or a full-time minister of God who seemed to have been rammed and battered by discouragement — and possibly a 'burnout'. Whether they are a spouse or a minister, either has had their fire ebbed lower and lower until it had gone dimmer — and dimmest! This soul probably had — at the onset of their spiritual or marital journey — charged for the crown of rejoicing as they put their hands into the plough. But somewhere along the way however, life's merciless strong currents had unmoored their ship from its bollard — and possibly gored them farther away from their intended destination. Or actually, had capsized their vessel!

The outcomes of events in your life do *not* necessarily have to fit the descriptions above; similar pressure accompany living daily life, if rightly seasoned with temperance had from time immemorial always built up a winning athlete's muscles!

A godly home for instance has a godly woman working hard to build up her home to her taste — even though the scripture teaches God as the ultimate Builder of marital bliss! But He ordained the wife in the home as *the minister*; first, to Him, her husband, children — and herself, in that order. That's God's order for the wife in the home: She is first and foremost, God's *minister* in that home!

You've often heard it said: *"Beside every successful*

husband is his wife!" Same it is in our christian vocation: No married minister's anointing could be efficiently stoked without the erstwhile support of his wife! Argue with me if you will, but that's just the way God had ordained it to be! That's God's mandate: The wife's unhindered companionship emotionally, sexually — and otherwise imparts the anointing of her husband!

Without doubt, if the fire in your belly must keep burning, battle axes of the Lord do need to strike, somewhat, *that* necessary balance necessary both to stoke and maintain *the* fire! We mandatorily need to 'balance up' work and play; social and spiritual activities, mentoring and being mentored — plus separating quality family time from disciplined work ethics (including attending to telephone calls and text messages) in order to observe quality times with our spouses! It is at such times that the ministers do indeed *minister* to each other's bodies, souls and spirit! Remember the Lord Jesus Christ had done exactly that, with His own disciples? Saint Mark recorded: *"He ordained twelve, that they should be with him ..."* | Mark 3:14. Intimacy of couple-ministers in the midst of busy, daily schedule of modern-day living is essential, if their fires would not grow dim! I found it most interesting to have penned these very words as an integral part of my keen observation of my hosts — the Taylors, when I'd stayed at their cottage.

In all honesty, it wasn't a cottage; but rather, a two-bedroomed open-living, kitchen-diner-upstairs and a huge basement that had boasted of its own huge living room, *en-suite* bedroom, a lavish office and a wash room. They had gracefully vacated the master bedroom which boasted of an ornate, Cherrywood-carved king-sized bed for the slightly smaller second bedroom.

Kat had been lavish and opulent in her hospitality, cleanliness, interior design and home décor tastes. Both the couple and I had shared the same restroom; even that had been sparkling and immaculate! Oh my, drawing comparisons between theirs and ours in England had been quite easy: Ours had been shared between five teenagers and I; theirs, between themselves and their two sons past adolescence — who had fled the nest! I had ensured that restroom — which in England we refer to as the 'loo' if you're trying to be posh (or simply 'toilet' if you hailed from the Old School) — had been scrubbed, mopped clean and perfumed as I'd met it, each time I had had occupied it the entire tenure of my sojourn! Later, I would learn a testimony from the couple how the Lord had achieved a major healing in the pastor's wife in the area of excessive decontamination-practices!

The restroom apart, the rest of their home was homely and welcoming. The Canadians have a saying: *"If our hearts are opened to receive you, so also is our home."*

Not only had Dr. Katarina *ministered* hospitality — and a welcoming home, she also had ministered through her stupendous culinary abilities. She'd treated her family — and this happy guest — to a table that could have been totally mistaken for a state-banquet. It had only been short of the fanfare and press-coverage accorded celebrities. She had practiced her hospitality in light of eternity's perspective. Even as I wrote this page, I can only be forever grateful to this wonderful couple for having afforded me the sheer privilege offered me.

The following morning when I had shared with her my deepest appreciation, she had confessed to me in a one-to-one conversation: *"My ministry first and foremost; is to God, followed by taking care of my husband's needs — all of them!"* And I'd nodded in perfect synchrony! Blessed beyond comparison is that wife who recognizes that God specially created wives to be partners — ministers of the grace of God — in the proclamation of the Goodnews. It certainly isn't hard for a godly husband like my friend, to realize he's been well-favored of the Lord!

Men and women are wired quite distinctly separately by the Creator God. Our needs therefore — and the methods through which we affirm each other —

are very fundamentally as different, as there are individuals irrespective of whether or not we are ministers! Four major areas of *any* husband's needs that must be ministered to by the wife therefore are: *Respect, sex, friendship* and *domestic helpfulness* in that order. And for the wife: *Security, honest communication, non-sexual affection* (including words of affirmation and acts of affection) — and *leadership* in that order. Any man that could boast of meeting these four needs in the life of a damsel is *the* sure deal.

An additional area that ranks equal with the need for sex in most men is the necessary boulevard to the stomach: It has to be a freeway — free of unwanted traffic. Therefore, an essential area of expertise a godly wife exerts the pressure to develop winning muscles in order to be the *minister*-keeper of her husband is in culinary arts and an outstanding expertise in the kitchen department!

"But my husband also does excellent dishes too," Dr. Katarina had quipped! Despite the fact that she holds four different college / university degrees and a full-time secular work, Kat is down to earth, both outside — and within the home. She certainly is a pilot truly very much at ease in her cockpit. She had before my departing England for theirs asked especially what my feeding habits were. That conversation on

the phone could very much have been likened to an informal interview. She had *not* left anything out to eventualities; I had later learned from her husband that she had at a time been a near perfectionist. Born in former Yugoslavia and having lived in Canada for over three decades, Kat blended her taste of western cooking with the culinary advances of Eastern Europe and the Mediterranean.

"How could I indulge your appetite with food?;" she'd requested. She also had reminded me to be very sincere, and honest.

I had been truthful and sincere. I had informed her that I'm a light eater; I had always been since my youth. So I had requested plenty of natural fruits and veg., some fibers and some hake fish. I could feast on those all-day, all week, all month, all year — not forgetting my crazy nuts: Almond, cashew, pistachio, walnuts and Brazil nuts. *"Avocado is my natural substitute for butter which I haven't eaten in as many years as over three decades"* I'd not forgotten to mention!

My dietary requirements *had* been well documented. When I'd arrived at their home; she had presented me a copy of a neatly hand-written note of every conversation we had had on the phone — including that of my feeding preferences. That had riveted to the very core of my spirit: *Meticulousness in hospitality*. I think every host / hostess should develop that essential quality so much wanton in major profiteering restaurants! These days of food-allergies with grievous consequences if faltered, the minister of hospitality would do well to take heed to the individual feeding preferences of their guest(s).

The couple had taken me on a quick tour of the basement and the upper chamber of their home. The tour had concluded at the dining area. Kat had shown me the cabinets – and opened wide, the huge, granite-colored, American refrigerator and said theatrically with the wave of a hand and a bow: *"All yours, Doc., all contents, yours!"* My mind had snapped. I had blinked — and quickly remembered Solomon's injunction in *Proverbs 23:1-3*. How could anyone *not* remember that? I personally wouldn't ever forget to be considerate in my appetite's yearnings when I had so much drilled same discipline into my five young children from infancy as my own parents had done us five or six decades earlier as they had raised us!

Even though none of my children had been allowed a sleepover-night at any of their friends' places, they still had been instructed to be considerable eaters anytime they had attended parties! No, *sleep-overs* just wasn't *my* thing. But here, the Taylors would make me remember for the rest of my life, my first-time stay at theirs. *"We're one big rejoiceful family in Christ"* they often chorused, ubiquitously.

Every servant of God requires at least one such faithful couple as ministry-friends — and partner — who could afford them lavish hospitality in a foreign space, out-looking foreign foods and culture until their spirit be re-kindled and refreshed. This was much akin to what gift of an attic-room or a chalet the wealthy Shunammite and her husband had offered Prophet Elisha in the story related to us in *2 Kings 4:8–11*. Well, I am grateful to God for my friends; the wife — in the presence of her husband — had repeatedly said: *"You would not require a hotel any time you arrived Canada, man of God. Our home is your home!"*

Wouldn't you too like to hear that?

After the 2015 Easter Sunday service, the crockery pot had mounted the hub as soon as we had arrived home! The sweet smelling aroma of a potpourri of meat, fish and condiments had pervaded the air. Kat had us treated to a steaming pot of rice pilaf, some large prawns and smoked-dry red meat. There were also some Canadian white fish (the particular name of which I couldn't exactly recall now. But I'm sure it hadn't been hake).

"You need to try something new and different every so often, Doc.," she had said in her beautiful Canadian accent.

I had smiled.

She had been right.

Her dish of pilaf-rice had been cooked in seasoned fish broth. Some red onion sliced in concentric rings as well as some mixed herbs and spices had perfected her intent. She'd also added some conspicuous bits and chunks of dried fruits. Olive oil and green vegetable had also attested to their attendance!

The second cuisine I had memory of was the *paulj*. Like you, I still have a slight complication pronouncing the tongue-twisting name. It was one of the delicacies Serbians would prepare for a *very* honorable guest.

Paulj is predominantly a bean soup; kidney beans to be exact, with some smoked goat meat. I had loved both cuisines — and had had my stomach ministered to in a great way.

How could I still write about these foods?

I could still write on these delicacies because my hosts had given me more than a reason to remember the words of our Lord Jesus Christ:

> *"He that receiveth you receiveth me, and he that receiveth me receiveth him that sent me.*
>
> *He that receiveth a prophet in the name of a prophet shall receive a prophet's reward; and he that receiveth a righteous man in the name of a righteous man shall receive a righteous man's reward.*
>
> *And whoever shall give to drink unto one of these little ones a cup of cold water only in the name of a disciple, verily I say unto you, he shall in no wise lose his reward."*
>
> | Matthew 10:40-42

If guest(s) departed your home or ministry — and could afford to forget the quality of your food fed them and the remarkability of your hospitality, both your kitchen and hospitality departments must be shambolic — and begging for a complete overhaul!

That had not been my experience at all in Canada. My hosts had ensured it had been a perfectly wonderful Easter celebration; one which I would never *ever* forget. Possibly, that as well had been their intent! No one could have asked for more!

In today's clergy circles where traditional hospitality has become almost a forgotten ministry, we must guard against forgetting that hospitality is a worthy ministry that synergizes with the pulpit ministry, thus enhancing the Word preached with greater impact! In fact, God's word commands us to be *"a lover of hospitality"* in *Titus 1:8*. Hospitality is the ministry of the unsung heroes and heroines. It is a ministry that comes willingly from the heart. That's why in many references in the scripture, the exact phrase *"given to"* had suffixed *"hospitality"* | *See Romans 12:7-8 & 1 Timothy 3:2*. We must be a people of the Word: "given to hospitality" both for His name-sake and ours!

Your life — and/or ministry has neglected her place of primary assignment if she least prioritizes, or is *not* given to hospitality. The consequences of such a neglect sometimes may be subliminal; other times, quite outrageous in every ramification. When the crockery pot is on fire however, intent on manufacturing a rare cuisine for saintly consumption, both the beneficiaries and benefactors are blessed — one obviously being more blessed than the other! (*Cf. Acts 20:35*). Benefactors are rewarded more with such redounding blessing! This is in accordance with the teachings of scriptures.
Our God encourages us therefore, to *"not forget to entertain strangers"* for we may unknowingly be refreshing God's angels in the act |*See Hebrews 13:2*.

Watch this: Any business entity, community, church or home wherever hospitality has been used *"one toward another without grudging"* as the Apostle Peter admonishes, thereupon rests undeniable tremendous blessings | *1 Peter 4:9*.

Wherever the crockery pot of hospitality comes on fire, the outpour from it warms hearts and minds: A fire is lit that ultimately transmits into the spirit, inextinguishably!

Why then wouldn't you put a crockery pot on fire, today?

CHAPTER FIVE

Live; On Fire: *'Never Done this Before!'*

5
T Live; On Fire: *'Never Done this Before!'*

The tension anticipating appearing on a live, worldwide telecast had been more than real but some of that built-up pressure had been released, thank God, in part; due to the distensible ministry of hospitality of my friends. They had taken time off their busy schedules and accosted me across the Ambassador Bridge, the busiest international trade-volume border crossing in continental North America. A tall suspension bridge over River Detroit, it handles just about a quarter of all merchandise trading between Canada and the USA. It was a stricter regime on the American side, than the Canadian, in my opinion. The border agent had demanded for our passports — and upon learning that I held a British passport had been just a little bit curious. But I had nothing to hide. Among the series of questions he had asked had been why I had preferred to enter the USA via Canada and not flown directly to Detroit. Well, I hope you as well by now could have answered him on my behalf. To be honest, I had even volunteered him some information that I'd once passed through the Niagara frontier border into the USA for a mere three-day visit a few years previous, owing to the sort of expedition I engage in! It was when he'd heard that that he had acquiesced! He'd then mentioned his love for the English Premiership — and intimated he had traveled to England a few years ago just to watch his favorite team, Manchester United play in the Premiership finals which they had won. At that, we both seemed to finally have touched base! He had returned my passport — and had wished us well!

I tell you, a friend's presence is golden at such unexpected, un-nerving moments: But I actually had two for comfort. Dr. Taylor had manned the driving wheel; he had driven his beautiful wife and I to the television station's headquarters in Detroit, Michigan.

The *Total Christian Television* station's executive manager, Bob Gross had requested us to have been seated three-quarters of an hour before the commencement of the live broadcast. We had arrived an hour-and-a-half earlier! It seemed like my customary attitude. I'd always loved turning up at meetings much earlier; I just loved to soak up the atmosphere of venues I'd been requested to speak at, if foreign or strange to me. I had most often times walked around the facility in disguise; some other times, I had approached the technicians — and asked questions about their acoustics, set-up's and so on. I had *not* needed to pull from my silly hat any of my silly pranks this day. All had seemed set to very high standards! We had been met by a cordial receptionist who had asked for our identification, each; before motioning us to sign their Fire Register. The producer, a very sharp-looking, mid-thirty-ish, African-American brother, Michael Hargrove had shepherded our group — and two other guests into the "Green Room". Here, he had most professionally handled our briefing — and very quickly given us the cues: *Our* individual cues! Then he had added: *"This is live television, y'all; if you happen to make a mistake, just don't worry. You must carry on as if it was normal, because it is normal! Even professionals make mistakes. I just thought I needed to chip that in."* That had been an angelic, very personal message to me. (I doubted if Mr. Hargrove had realized it?)

Soon, we had had real opportunities to meet the camera-crew and a few others who had been on duty that evening. Dr. Sam Mallete had reported the viewers' written-in testimonies — and he and I had actually shared some banter before we had gone on air. I had even nosed in at the prayer counselors' room. They were all a professional lot. Messers. Gregory Butler's and Jay Kilburn's names and faces I would never forget: One wore a perfectly smooth-shaved face; the other a perfectly shaved-head that tapered into a huge goatee! These gentlemen had made us all feel at home. The former had mastered the cameras and the latter had pinned up and adjusted our microphones to the different speakers' voice-pitches.

I had chosen the option of a lavalier mic. as opposed to a hand-held microphone because of my incurable gesticulation habits. I had always cherished the freedom of using my hands to aid my communication. Some seminarians advice their audience: *"A speaker must stay still behind a pulpit, look to the two divergent angles in the audience and make eye-contacts to effectively deliver."* I say I could — and on many occasions had sat on the steps leading up to the altar, no bible in hand and delivered many a perfect homily from that vantage position of vulnerability. No listener's eyes could ever fail to glue onto such a preacher! Anyway, I advocate Prophet's Samuel counsel to Saul of Kish: *"Do as occasion bids you once the oil is on your head!"*

Not only had we the opportunity to familiarize ourselves with the excellent staffers and other guests present at *TCT–TV* that evening, I'd also 'tested' the cameras. The thought of those luminous lights and the huge recording lenses all about to roll ubiquitously focused on me on a live international broadcast suddenly had given me the chills! (Remember, I had never done this before.) My lips had dried up despite an earlier application thinly, of a lip balm. My throat too had followed suit. Granted, a couple of years previous, I'd been *the* 'trainee' on my own program: *'Harvestways with Sammy Joseph.'*

'Harvestways with Sammy Joseph' is the media flagstaff of our ministries. It tapes, edits and produces our then fifteen-minute, weekly video teachings across the world. For thirty months: March 2013 — September 2015, God favored us to partner with an international radio station in northern California — Radio Pan Am. They broadcast to the world 24/7. We had chosen to broadcast to West Africa with an estimated 212 million-listening audience, twice weekly on the shortwave radio — and thrice weekly on their internet radio. Through this medium, many had come to relate with Jesus Christ as their personal Lord and Savior. Many more had referred to me as their 'radio pastor.' They had written in and asked for materials to help them grow. Books had been freely sent as we had deemed

most befitting their individual needs. Despite this seed-planting thrust, our understanding had been that lesser than 3% of listeners to most religious radio broadcasts do actively send in financial support to continue with such broadcasting. Unfortunately as our experience had proven, lesser than 0.00001% of our estimated listeners had at any one month supported us. With the speculations surrounding the national referendum on Brexit early 2016 very rife, the purchasing power of the £GB (British Pound Sterling) had begun to slide down unsavorily from an average all-time stable £1.60GBP to the $USD in winter of 2015, to £1.40 at first — and then further down in spring of 2016 on the Foreign Exchange Markets (*FOREX*). By June, the £GB pound had slid further down to £1.21 to the $US Dollar. She had jollied at the same spot ever since. The £ GBP had acquired her all-time low status in thirty-five years on the world's currency market. This had translated just one fact: Other world currencies had been stronger than the British Pound Sterling! That had availed our exports (British goods) much cheaper — and affordable to the world, while imports (or foreign purchases) had become dearer to the British consumers. We had thought it wise to cut back on our mounting costs on the exchange rate markets. We had been forced to discontinue our partnership with the station and staff we so much loved!

We had received consolation from the Lord, directives to concentrate our efforts chiefly on the production of DVD's — and a continued broadcasting in *HD* format, messages uploaded onto the YouTube, freely. Our channel would bear the name: *HarvestWays*. We had ceased paid radio broadcast in the interim!

God never promoted any further or higher above and beyond their preparatory foundation. The fire in a child of God constantly needed being fanned into burning, blue, tongue-flames through the very muscle-building blocks we loath. Yet, it should be counted a privilege to experience pressure presented us through life's adversities and challenges! These are the character-forming blocks Heaven employs from time immemorial!

Some of my broadcasting muscle-ripples had been formed partly from becoming a humble "trainee" on *my* own show as earlier noted. My apprenticeship with the Holy Spirit had lasted roughly about two years — even though it is still ongoing! I had started recording with the aid of a tiny *Sony* handy-camcorder. (The very first sets of messages recorded are still evident at our *HarvestWays* YouTube channel!) Soon, the Lord had granted us ownership of the very first high-definition SONY professional camera and a set of 2 x 600-wattage halogen lights! Our incorporation of a very sensitive *AKG* ulta-high frequency lavalier-mic. had tremendously boosted the sound quality of the broadcast. Gradually, faithful subscribers had started paying attention to the message heaven had sent me. People who had watched from as far as the Far East, Australia and the North Americas had begun writing in. They had shared tremendously how the Lord had blessed them through the messages. I have told this same story ever since — and I am not shy to tell it here, once again: My backside-of-the-desert preparation had undoubtedly gotten me in a topnotch form for such a time as the night of April 2, 2015 in Detroit, Michigan where I had faced the entire world. Sitting behind that brown oak dining-table on *'Harvestways with Sammy Joseph'* under 1200-wattage lights gazed upon by a single lens had at that time demanded a feat of sweaty palms and repeated cues of 'Start-Stop-Now-Start-again producer-orders'. A fifteen-minute message had been achievable *only* after four hours of frustrating ordeal, taping. As a young lad, I had suffered from perfectionist tendencies. I must admit I hadn't curbed that tendency in those earlier days of broadcasting training! For me, everything had to be near-perfect — if not cute perfect! Facing however those three giant round lenses in the *TCT-TV* studio all blinking at different times had almost given me a panic attack! My unedited message would be relayed live to 100 million North American homes (including Canada) — and as many as 170 nations of the world, in an instant! That kind of production had been totally alien to me!

To worsen issues, I had just being informed — credits to misinterpreted information passed onto me by our liaisons department — I would be speaking for half an hour instead of an hour I had prepared for. That had meant just one thing: Ditch the former sermon with its embellishments and jokes which had been thoroughly researched to suit the Michiganders whose impression of, reactions to — and acceptance (or otherwise) of my personality I'd been completely unsure of! I had had only twenty minutes to produce an equally befitting twenty-five minute message.

What would you have done under such a circumstance?

The same question I had asked the Holy Spirit within me. I had *not* panicked — but had been intent on paying close attention to His still small voice. Oh, He had tapped into the depth of my study in my most alone-times with Him. And surely I had heard these words:

> *"Re-tell the story of Abraham's encounter with the three angels in Genesis 26. Link it with God's ban of the Ammonites and the Moabites from ever entering the congregation of the Lord to their tenth*

generation — indeed, forever! Title this sermon: Barrier-Breakers!"

Yes, that had been *it!* My spirit had suddenly switched to over-drive. I had scribbled like a chicken onto the sides my sermon notebook, highlighting one or two biblical references! This message would be delivered against the backdrop of the four red-blood lunar appearances of 2015 — the last of which was about to occur April 4th, two days after this broadcast! Another link in the message would be a solid reflection on the rumors of the United States' Supreme Court's deliberation on *Obergefell v. Hodges*. It had been rumored that the deliberation had been tilted to favor same-sex marriages and civil-partnerships in America! That case had been scheduled for an April 28, 2015 hearing.

It was certain the Lord would not have me pull no punches on the issues surrounding the *LGBT*. Rather, His Spirit would open both my eyes and ears to know what to say — and when to say it, as the sermon progressed! As a prophet, I see open visions. But I also hear from time to time *"the word of the Lord via the invisible hearing loops connected my ears"*, as I often say! These two gifts of the Spirit are some of the manifestations of the gifts of prophecy.

The studio atmosphere had been electric; you could feel the charge in the air! The producer, the evening's staff and we had said a quick prayer of agreement. Our host had been the legendary Dr. Dorinda Clarke-Cole, an accomplished evangelist and a singer of the famed *Coles*; three-time Grammy award winner and of the recent *Preachers of Detroit*. Once the camera lights had switched onto LIVE, she had also prayed. She had been soft-spoken, highly polished — and full of gait and grace! The cue for the *Celebrate* show had been strictly implemented: One of *The Greater Emmanuel Institutional Church of God in Christ* adjutants, Kim Miller would be engaged in a fifteen-minute interview, having being preceded by the master saxophonist, Jeremy Cornelius' number: *Running Back to You*. He had played this jazzy, five-minute track as the intro to his musical prodigy!

His second number *Outpour* would usher in Dr. Cole's introduction of me as the preacher of the night on the half-hour mark! *Outpour* had been precisely timed and chosen by the Holy Spirit. It had been preparatory; prayer-like, a powerfully prophetic, alto-sax piece played on the background track of vocalists who had prayed the Spirit of God to send down His power in repetitive refrain: *"Send it down!"*

That prayerful piece had ushered me personally, unto Heavenly realms. Then Dr. Cole had stepped up to the glass pulpit — and with her characteristic, buoyant smile had introduced me to "commandeer" the last hour of preaching the word and ministrations; thus:

> *"And now I'm really happy because it's time for the Word of God. You know we can't live without the Word. We can't walk without the Word, we can't speak without the Word; it's the Word of God that really penetrates our hearts — and allows us to live this christian life. And I am so grateful and so honored to have all the way from Birmingham.*
>
> *Wait a minute, y'all didn't catch that. Y'all didn't catch that ... I want you all to help me welcome all the way from Birmingham, England; Author, Pastor, Dr. Sammy Joseph.*
>
> *You take it away — and let the Lord use you!"*

With an *"Amen; God bless you! Halleluyah, I'll do that"*, I had responded to Dr. Cole's perfect introduction of me.

Then these exact words:

> *"I wanna thank God for the opportunity to come here tonight to speak the Word God has laid upon my heart from Birmingham, England. Let's just*

bow down our heads and pray, shall we?"

From that moment, the Holy Spirit had roared alive His engine on the inside of me into an unquenchable huge fireball:

> *"Father, we thank You so much for this grace that You've given us to share Your Word. I just ask Lord, that You begin to send forth to the airwaves the glory of Your Name; the power of Your resurrection.*
>
> *Draw us close to you Oh, God; You're all we need ... Thank You for Your Son that came to die on the Cross, 2000 years ago. We worship You for Your life You gave to us ...*
>
> *I pray tonight by the power of the Holy Spirit under this great influence and anointing; Oh, Lord; speak through me. Break bondages. Set men and women free. Let the phone lines be jammed tonight.*
>
> *We give you praise, in Jesus name. Amen — and amen."*

Every living oracle of God should be able to tell what kind of a "take-off" experience they had; whether it had been smooth, against gusty winds, jangling or bumpy. Here's what's worked for me time and again:

> *Say a short opening prayer committing your session into the hands of the Holy Spirit; take a back-seat — and watch him fly your plane, drive your car or power-pedal your bicycle, whichever yours is!*

Those simple words of prayer said on my very first live international television appearance had been prophetic! Once that had been accomplished, my takeoff had been smooth. I had relaxed and allowed the Lord be my Pilot. You know, I am grateful the Lord could use me to minister to you even through these printed pages, too. What a great privilege to be a razor — or at times, a quiet — mouthpiece for Heaven! Once you too have accorded Him His rightful place, the Holy Spirit wouldn't let your voice be *just* the voice of any other mortal man. Every word you utter would be lethally possessed by God. That's usually the difference between an orator and an oracle: One could stir your mind; the other, has a tremendous long-lasting impact upon your spirit!

Everyone could feel the supernatural presence of the Holy Spirit by the prevailing atmosphere in the studio that night. It had been super easy to teach, preach, exhort and prophesy — all within the time-limit. And God had confirmed His presence with undisputable signs, following.

I had spoken as directed by the Holy Spirit from *Deuteronomy 23:3-4*. Here, God had placed a ban of entry into the congregation of the Lord on the Ammonites and Moabites, up unto their tenth generation — even forever! Read the edict with me:

> *"An Ammonite and a Moabite shall not enter into the congregation of the LORD; even unto their tenth generation shall they not enter into the congregation of the Lord for ever."*

His holy fire in me had been stoked; it had billowed forth:

> *"That's interesting though — because they could not enter in!*
>
> *But there were some people that broke that barrier. Jesus Himself was a Barrier-Breaker! The Bible says in Ephesians, Chapter 2: 'He is our Peace.' He had had broken down the middle wall of partition between us and God. So there is no more Jew or Gentile. There's no more Greek or Roman; no more American or Japanese; we are all one in*

Christ Jesus because of the Blood shed for us!

Why would God put a ban on the entry of the Ammonites and the Moabites into the holy congregation?

'Because they met you (the Israelites) not with bread and with water in the way when you came out of Egypt.'

There are some people in our lives going through stuff. Notice with me very quickly, five or six attributes of barrier-breakers."

Major Attributes of Barrier-breakers

"Generally, barrier-breakers are:

a.) Merciful people: they do not burden the already burdened. Rather, they unburden the very burdens bound on folk! People who are barrier-breakers do not add more troubles on troubled souls. Rather, they are merciful to them. Jesus says in Matthew 5:

'To the merciful, he shall receive mercy.'

You wanna receive mercy tonight?

> *Be merciful. Help the broken. Raise them up by the power of the Holy Spirit. Encourage them. Give to them. Speak a word in season into their lives. Prophesy unto them.*
>
> *Yes, we all have stuff going on in our lives! Stuff that are not okay, sometimes; but in spite of that, the Bible requests of us to encourage one another and lift up one another in the things of God! You see, God was teaching us through the Ammonites and the Moabites to not deny helping those we have the power to help. These two tribes had the power to feed and succor the emancipated children of Israel when they had come close to their borders en-route Canaan. Instead, they had refused.*
>
> *Barrier-breakers are merciful people: They unburden burdens."*

I had just torn into the meat of my sermon. Very quickly, I had attacked the loins too, tracing the genealogy of the Ammonites and the Moabites as the grandsons of Lot.

> *"Back to the stories in Genesis, Ammon and Moab had been conceived the night Lot had been drunk and had engaged in incestuous sexual encounters with his daughters, unknowingly."*

I had explained the *theophany*: That is the appearance unto Abraham, Lot's Uncle, of Archangels Michael and Gabriel — and the Judge of all the earth, Jesus *en route* to the destruction of Sodom and Gomorrah!

> *"I believe that the Archangel Gabriel is coming to your home right now; tonight, ready to bring you Good News. He always brings good news. He was going to deliver Lot, his wife — and their daughters' families safely out of Sodom for the Bible says 'Lot was a righteous man' — despite the fact that he went through self-inflicted hardships.*
>
> *No matter what hardships you too go through tonight, I want you to know that God loves you; Jesus cares about you ... God says to Lot, you know, you could have made mistakes. You could have fought with Abraham on business prospects, cattle and finances; nevertheless, I still love you!*
>
> *God in Jesus — and in the presence of His two archangels: Michael and Gabriel — was descending upon Sodom and Gomorrah; an exact picture of events yet to occur in the end times.*
>
> *On the 4th of this month (April 2015), all over the world, we're gonna have another red blood moon! That ought to let you know the end is coming; like*

it or not!

Your arrows will not be able to stop Jesus' appearing in the sky. Your missiles will not be able to stop Him because He's the LORD of lords! Let me tell you something here tonight: Get ready for the appearance of Christ. Get ready! Get ready!!

Archangel Gabriel was sent to go rescue Lot. Our other friend, Archangel Michael was going to rain down fire and brimstone from Heaven, on Sodom and Gomorrah. Get it straight tonight; God hates sin but loves the sinner. Whatever you're doing in Sodom, God is not for you. America listen clearly tonight — the voice of God is coming into your homes through the radio-waves and the international waves. God is not against you. He loves you! He wants to help — and save you.

So in that story, we see Abraham had entreated the three men to be refreshed by him and Sarah. That brings me to the second point about Barrier-breakers! They are:

b.) Watchful of the spiritual – and ready to sacrifice unto God. People who are barrier-breakers are also going to be watchful; ready to offer costly sacrifices unto the Lord with all their heart, soul and mind.

'For thou shall love your God with all your heart, soul and mind — and your neighbor as yourself.'

Abraham was in a big mess: Old and possibly with a bald-patch like I do have; but he had no son — and he had wanted a son. He was very rich. He had servants and maidens. He had a rewarding job, a beautiful home and a pretty, smart wife. But he did not have a son. That had been the issue in his life!

Now, if you want what you've never got, you've gotta be willing to give what you've never given! So he said to Sarah: 'Honey, we've got an exigency! We've gotta prepare to receive some important guests. Can you please knead the flour and prepare the fatted calf?'

Thank God for a godly wife; thank God for Sarah! She went in — and began to prepare as her lord did ask of her. In the intervening time, Abraham and the Lord began to discuss. In their discussion, the Lord mentioned He and the other two were on a mission towards the Zoar valley where his nephew Lot and family resided, to destroy Sodom and Gomorrah.

You see, the Bible says the Lord God will do nothing except He had first intimated His ser-

vants the prophets | Amos 3:7.

The Lord had intimated Abraham that the cries and the stench of their sins had reached unto Heaven. He should have to send the judgment!

And here's the third thing Barrier-breakers would do:

c.) Negotiate and intercede for the land. Barrier breakers are expert negotiators! They negotiate to deliver the captives from the snares of the devil. So Abraham had struck a negotiating pact — and an intercessory post with the Lord God!

'If you found fifty righteous souls there, would you still destroy the land?' The Lord answered 'No'. 'What of forty?' 'No'. What of thirty? Same answer: 'No'.

Abraham got a bit embarrassed and entreated the Lord: 'Please don't be offended at my request, but what if you found twenty righteous people in Sodom, will you still destroy it?' And the Lord said 'No'.

You see, intercessors are needed for America today! Intercessors are needed to stay on their knees and

> *pray — and fight this battle. This battle belongs to the Lord of Hosts. That's His name. He will win this battle if we'd stay on our knees and pray:*
>
> *'If my people which are called by my name shall humble themselves …'*
>
> *Let's kneel and humble ourselves before God — 'and pray; and seek His face …' He will heal our land! Let's raise the altar to bring God's glory down, America! Let's bring down the glory on our children. On our homes. On our marriages. Even on that one that is running away from home. Let's kneel down and pray!"*

At this moment, I had instinctively found myself modeling the kneeling-position of prayer beside the glass pulpit, raising both hands to Heaven like the prophets of old had done. The liquid fire of God's Spirit had been felt in that studio.

> *"Instead of you cursing that child, you begin to intercede for the child. You begin to say 'I'm not gonna let my child go to the devil; no, no, no; you belong to the Lord. My children and I: We belong to the Lord — and we shall serve the Lord, the word of God says, America! Listen to the voice of God, tonight!"*

Then my tongue had begun to prophesy:

> *"There's one child that's ready to run away from home, I hear the voice of God talk to me right now. As I'm speaking, Archangel Gabriel is right there, right now to minister to you; don't be a runaway. Ask the Holy Spirit to draw you closer home. If you're that child the Holy Spirit is speaking to; pick that phone right now and dial the number you see at the bottom of the screen. God is speaking to you: You don't need to run away ..."*

Indeed, I still feel the anointing of the Lord upon these words right now — even as I write. You see, the anointing is transferrable. Same God, same Spirit is present on the pages of this book! Possibly you are contemplating running away too: You may *not* be a child; you may be a spouse, an under-worker, a staff at a business enterprise ready to call it quits. The term "runaway" is pregnant with many meanings and interpretations, spiritually and literally speaking. Doors may have been shutting in your face for a while; same repetitive doors also may have shut on your fore-fathers. They shut systematically — and you have nowhere else to turn. The Holy Spirit says *"Don't run away. Don't quit!"* Allow the same Holy Spirit to speak to your heart.

Fourthly, barrier-breakers:

d.) Entreat God. They fight. They wrestle with God. Scripture says of Jacob the cheat at Ford Jabbok that he wrestled with God: 'For as a prince, thou had power with God and with men, and thou hast prevailed' | Genesis 32:28.

Barrier-breakers could be wounded — and halt like Jacob, but like a bulldog, they would never let go! They'd say: 'You may drag me, but drag me with you into health. You may drag me, but drag me with you into wealth. You may drag me, just drag me with you into blessing. You may drag me but drag me with you into prosperity and opportunity. Just don't leave me the way you found me!

Is that your story, tonight?

e.) Lastly, barrier-breakers would acknowledge their issue(s) — and laugh in the face of them. Never you give up, cave in or quit at the face of any issue; help is at hand. The glory of the Lord will be revealed against such bondages and afflictions. They will assuredly melt away when confronted by the power of the Holy One of Israel! Confess and declare unto the Lord in simple sentence the issues you battle with.

> *It could be you're held under the bondage of addiction to a sin, I may not tell! All I assuredly can tell is that help is at hand, tonight!"*

> *The Lord and His two archangels were readily set on the Sodom and Gomorrah mission. Abraham revealed his dire need to the Lord. He said: 'Lord, I have an issue; Sarah has still not had the child You promised, twenty-four years ago!' The Lord had replied: 'According to earth's calendar; this time next year, she shall have a son.' But Sarah laughed in mockery and unbelief! When confronted by the Lord, she did equally deny ever laughing!*

> *Now it doesn't matter whether your laughter was of disbelief or utter mockery, I said you will be pregnant and have a son; his name shall be called Isaac: Meaning, 'Laughter!'*

Again, the Spirit of prophecy had overcome me. So I had spoken forth these exact words:

> *"Somebody is going to laugh here tonight. God has sent me to speak to you. Take a moment to ask the Lord, 'Help me!'*

> *This time next year, I am praying for those of you who are barren — but would love to bear the*

fruit of the womb: You will carry your child. As a prophet, God has anointed me specially to pray like I am about to, for fertility in conception. I have ministered like this in Canada, America, South Africa, Nigeria, Ghana, and in the United Kingdom. Wherever I have prayed, shut wombs had been opened with twins!

You see, I am a father of multiple twins myself: I've got two sets of twins! You will conceive, except you don't want twin-babies. Not only am I gonna pray for those who want to be fruitful but also those who have no jobs; folk troubled with financial instability and insecurity. I will pray tonight and two jobs will be chasing you …

And oh, for those who are looking up unto the Lord for godly spouses. Suddenly, two men will show up and begin to pursue you: 'That girl's mine; she's mine, let's go on a date tonight' they will say. It's gonna happen by the power of the Holy Spirit right here, tonight!

Bow down your head and pray with me, will you?"

I had almost prayed when the Lord had revealed unto me a peculiar man in an open vision. I had described his exact details in the word of wisdom, thus:

> *"There's a particular man watching. You're bitter in your heart. You're very bitter. You're about sixty-two years old. You have your hair thinning out; I can see you. You went through a divorce over twenty-five years ago — and you never went back to see those children. Your daughter in particular is messed up. Really messed up big time; but she wants her daddy back. You're in Detroit and your family is partly on the west coast, very far away. Are you gonna heed these words and save your children? If you go and see those children and say to your daughter in particular: 'Baby, forgive me. I wanna be in your life', you will help heal the mental torments in that young lady's life. Tonight is your night."*

Then another word of knowledge had shot forth:

> *"There's someone right out there, with a growth on the inside. I can feel it in my belly. You're scheduled for an operation. Place your hand on your tommy. In the name of the Lord Jesus Christ, such growths are going to shrink. Watch what will come out from between your legs.*
>
> *If that's you, call the number on the screen now."*

Only then had I finally felt the release in my spirit to

pray thus:

> *"Father, I come to You in the name of Jesus Christ of Nazareth: I ask for double portion. Wombs, conceive! And you that are jobless, receive a double portion; in Jesus name. Amen.*
>
> *Maybe you don't even know Jesus Christ as your Lord and Savior, say with me now:*
>
> *'Father, in the name of Jesus Christ, I give myself to you. Come into my heart and save my soul in the name of Jesus Christ. Amen.'"*

The host, studio manager — and producer had thanked the Lord for His word that *"had cut through the multi-faceted strata of the American existence"*. Very quickly, the executive manager had asked me to *"let me know anytime you would visit the United States again as we would be more than privileged to extend our hands of fellowship to you to minister for us. Just give us a two-week notice!"*

Different prayer counselors had waved their hands through the separating glass panel, beckoning me to pray for them at the expiry of the broadcast. And I had! Their baseline confirmation had a common tone: *"There's been an unusual surge in the volume of callers on tonight's broadcast; our telephone lines had been fully jammed!"*

"All the glory is the Lord's" I had replied, casually, with a tired smile!

We had crossed back into Canadian territory as soon as I had completed 'dropping the word', like Prophet Ezekiel would have described it. It had been a successful debut; one which the ripple-effects of such a magnanimous anointing would be felt for many more weeks! One Marguerite Bird — a prayer counselor on duty that night — had not forgotten to send us a word even after I had arrived back in England. She had summed up the spirit of the aftermath of our encounter on their station:

> *"We had kept on taking calls of special, unusual testimonies, for the next fortnight after your departure!"*

Tongues of fire had been kindled in Detroit. I pray these billow forth through to the nations, in the name of the Lord!

Chapter Six
Fire at Harrow

6

Fire at Harrow

The sole objective of the special oil upon the minister's head is probably farthest from any figment of *your* imagination! They are intimated, the anointing on them was *not* intended them by the Giver for their monopolistic tendencies, or extravagancies! Rather, that precious oil is for serving those to whom they have been sent. If the minister has fully discharged this unction however, I am fully persuaded the residue should be subject to their discretion to use, with wisdom. The Word reminds us:

> *"And the spirits of the prophets are subject to the prophets."*
>
> | 1 Corinthians 14:32

Most often times, people would love to meet with a minister after an outpouring. There's nothing wrong with that. Only the carrier of the anointing *ought* to be able to tell when it was time to retreat from the people so as to be able to rest and re-charge before another outpouring! It should be the norm for a long lasting effective ministry.

My aim in this book is *not* to teach on preserving the anointing; that could as well be the title of another entire project. However, I shall endeavor to make accessible to you, tips on preserving *your* anointing — so you may last long!

Therefore, once all had been accomplished in Detroit, my body had begun to retreat. By the grace of God's super-enablement, we had successfully ticked the first box on mission *International Experience Harvestways Conference 2015*. My main sessions at Harrow, Ontario, Canada would begin the Good Friday morning — barely ten hours later. I *had* needed rest, crucially!

I am very blessed to have always been a quick sleeper. The lines must have fallen onto me in pleasant places; yea, surely I indeed have a goodly heritage. My dad too — during his sojourn on earth could sleep at a combined thousand locomotive engine-noises! My mom had not been so fortunate.

Some preachers suffer insomnia: The proofs are the puffs that have taken residence under their lower eyelids. The Lord had never allowed me to suffer sleeplessness at any given time in my life! Not even while I had raised my five children. Actually, none of them had ever awoken through a night's sleep. I know that would surprise you, but it's nevertheless true. That had been another testimony I had shared time — and time again! Anyway, nothing on earth had ever troubled my sleep. Maybe partly because I'd endeavored to ensure no troubled thought comes within my abode — let alone into my bedroom space, nor invade my mind-space. Other partly, because my spirit had over the years trained my mind to be at ease — and not stress.

Hence, I couldn't have remembered anything that had transpired on the journey from the United States back into Canada that triumphant April 2, 2015 night!

As I settled in the seat behind the couple in the car, I vaguely remember Dr. Kat advise her husband of the need to lower his voice so as *not* to rouse me awake!

Bless her!

My friend had nudged me back to consciousness once the car had parked in the garage. With some groceries in one hand, Dr. Alden had held the heavy mahogany door that had led from the garage into the lobby, with the other hand. I had bounced through the door, giving him a dull wink; and off I had gone straight up into bed. I hadn't even changed my wears. I remembered shoving my brown brogues, someplace in *my* room!

I had first opened my eyes at past 6 *a.m.* on Good Friday as soon as the alarms on my phones had blared! Birds had chirped and tweeted happily away in the morning, across the open field. The air had smelt freshly autumnal. I'd yawned and stretched on the king-sized, hand-carved, ornament bed meant for a king!

Thank God, I had had my messages prepared before departing England! I didn't want to get up — but had *had* to: Harrow Conference would commence 10 *a.m.* My hosts had been up, preparing: I had heard my friend in the adjacent room — and smelt a waft of toasted bread drift into mine, from the ledge beneath the door!

I would worship the Lord first, any day my pair of eyelids had parted open! As I'd begun to show gratitude unto the Lord, I'd heard the Holy Spirit speak to me:

> *"You will not preach that sermon you prepared to speak today until another day. Speak on a new one:*

'The Price of Betrayal' from Matthew's gospel, chapter twenty-one!"

That had been the order from my Unseen Executive Director. He always runs *my* shows. Would you believe that I am yet to preach the sermon He forbade me preaching up until this present day?

Never in my life had I ever stepped up to a podium or pulpit to deliver the word of the Lord without an adequate preparation bathed in prayers, fasting — and documentation thoroughly written out in my burgundy sermon notebook. That always had been my style. That sermon journal goes with me everywhere I had ever been. Regardless of my level of study however, the Lord may not allow me to open that sermon journal; rather, His Spirit would sensitize and alert me to the pressing needs of my different audiences.

Why does He sometimes do this to me?

I have asked Him many times, too. Maybe He would reveal His reason(s) to me in Heaven. Even at this, I am aware there are ministers who travel with their old sermon notes only to just 'open up' and 'dust up' a sermon preached years ago — and deliver the goods. You may never be able to tell the difference between a stale and fresh feed. But Heaven would tell — and reward them accordingly at Christ's Seat of judgment! This, the scripture teaches!

Preachers differ one to another — and I may *not* be doing you any justice recommending to you the best approach to arriving at a perfect *homiletics* or *hermeneutics*. Again, that's *not* my aim in this project! My tool-kit always had consisted of a copy of KJV bible (same common *King James Version* of the Bible that I call 'my study bible' because it has all the notes of my personal meditation with the Holy Spirit for at least two decades); a copy of Strong's Concordance — and a sermon journal! Other commentaries had always been used — but had not been airborne with me for the very obvious reason. I travel light you see, but these three had always formed the *belly* of my hand luggage. Then I always had handy too, a ball point pen in my coat pocket — in addition to one or two new, never-read books.

This Good Friday morning, I'd rolled over to the other side of the bed, yawned — and stretched again. But I'd been deeply convinced the Holy Spirit had some urgent, timely thing to say. My job would be to transcribe His dictation.

I love preparing sermons. I love studying. I certainly don't hate researching materials, facts and figures.

Thank God for the advent of the internet; these days, anyone could find out any piece of information at the snap of two fingers! I enjoy writing — and documenting. I journal whatever the Holy Spirit says to me. I've had a few times folks who had wanted to see proof or evidence of what I had preached. It had been very easy to respond appropriately to such non-threats. Your sermon-journal, voice or video-recording of messages could save your neck in case you had 'landed' before a court of law. Very much like a teacher's lesson plan, our record-keeping too are legal documents for the angels, the demons — and the world at large to see.

Scripture mandates, we *"must be ready to preach the Gospel"* | Romans 1:15. The emphasis is on the word 'ready'. We were advised to:

> *"Sanctify the Lord God in your hearts: And be ready always to give an answer to every man that asks you a reason of the hope that is within you with meekness and fear."*
>
> |1 Peter 3:15

Not only do I love to write out my sermons as proofs, I do so to keep track of what the Lord's Spirit had spoken to me in the past, with relevance to the present. Finally, I keep journaling my sermons because I could decide someday to publish them in volumes aimed as a study tool to bolster the confidence of younger batch of ministers of the Lord!

So like a scribe, I had written down every word the Holy Spirit had spoken unto my inner ears that very morning. After I had blessed the meal of the Word, it had been time to feast! Preparing an average fifty-minute delivery usually calls for a loyal, undivided half an hour-attention — or thereabouts! The Word of God is the well of life from which I draw with my spiritual pitcher! Years of dedicated comparative study of the Word is a blessed asset. Moments of storytelling — whether they be personal, experiential or another's gathered in counseling — would always keep listeners awake and alert. Therefore, from a heart well fed by the Holy Spirit, I had opened the conference in Harrow after having being so honorably introduced by Dr. Alden Taylor:

"Good morning!

I bring you bountiful glad tidings from my beloved family — and church family in Birmingham, England in the precious name of the Lord, Jesus Christ. I also do want to thank my friends — your pastors — for arranging this wonderful opportunity for me to bring you the Word! Yesterday evening as the pastor has noted, we saw the glory of the Lord revealed in Detroit; this morning, I believe the Holy Spirit is going to reveal unto us more of His person, will and acts during this service. So I want you to be expectant — very expectant of the fire from Heaven, falling upon us!

I shall be speaking to you this Good Friday morning; briefly, on the topic: 'The Price of Betrayal', from the twenty-first chapter of Matthew's gospel.

Here, we read of the major last events in the life of Jesus on earth. The last words of any dying person are very important both to himself and the loved ones soon to be bereaved! Last words or acts usually leave indisputable clues, hints and instructions on how they would love their legacy to be treated.

Last words in ancient times were orally binding. The departing patriarch would with wisdom arrest the attention of his children by convening a family meeting. At this crucial meeting, he / she addresses his / her children — and passes down the blessing!

The firstborn male child in most medieval cultures of the time was destined to become the heir to the father. He would be charged with the sole responsibility of executing his requests after his death.

Today, the process is less traumatic — particularly if the matriarch or patriarch had him / herself a will in place; written in black and white, safekept with a lawyer or solicitor in the Wills & Probate Department. A lot of family feud and animosities would be easily eliminated were parents encouraged to not die intestate! Likewise, our Lord Jesus Christ had left us a will in His Word, the Bible. More, He had also concisely left His eleven disciples who had succeeded Him, His very last words — and actions!

Shall we therefore consider some of the last words and deeds of the Lord Jesus Christ in His last week on earth?

a.) His triumphant entry into Jerusalem on a donkey:
This had signified the humility of the servant-King of kings!

'All this was done, that it might be fulfilled which was spoken by the prophet, saying: Tell ye the daughter of Zion, Behold, thy King cometh unto thee; meek, and sitting upon an ass, and a colt the foal of an ass.'
 | Matthew 21: 4-5 & Zechariah 9:9

Jesus Christ's entry into Jerusalem had been widely heralded throughout the city because God had masterfully and carefully orchestrated it:

'And when he was come into Jerusalem, all the city was moved, saying, Who is this? And the multitude said, This is Jesus the prophet of Nazareth of Galilee.'
| Matthew 21:10-11

In a day of fast 'n furious, iron-cladded rule of the brutal Romans, many had envisaged the Savior-Emancipator to arrive with fiery sets of eyes, pomp and gallantry upon blazing chariots! But no; the Son of God wouldn't bow to the pressure of acclaim in a show of power. The time for that showdown had been scheduled for a not-too-distant future!

His glorious entry into the capital city therefore wasn't penned down for a show. Rather, it would depict the humility of the servant King.

- *The question this affords you and I is: 'Is your life, living and calling a show for public rating and approval — or a demonstration of the leadership example set by the Lord to be the servant of all?'*

b.) His uprooting hedonism out of the Temple:

Jesus had made a great impression upon the multitudes of people when He had entered the city. But He also had so suddenly switched onto correcting an anomaly in the Temple!

What could that have been?

The anomaly had been the traders' disdain for God's holy habitation! The Son of God had displayed His raw passion to fix the aberration! He had displayed publicly, His strong disapproval of them that had traded in the temple; He'd overthrown the tables of the fat-bellied, profiteering, money-changers. He had yanked the stools off of the bottoms of those that had cheated the very poor in the money-changing dove trade!

I could envisage some by-standers who had witnessed Him arrive Jerusalem just under an hour ago fold their arms across their chests in absolute stupendous horror! Some had their eyeballs as big as plates when they had witnessed the supposed King of the Jews display outlandish anger in the holy place.

But the Lord hadn't just been irate without a focus! The object of His wrath had been the desecration of the temple of God; a far cry from its intended, sole aim as the "house of prayer for all nations." That had been prophesied by Prophets Isaiah and Jeremy; but the traders had transformed the temple of God into a den of robbers!

It has been said that when the sole reason for the existence of a thing is unknown, abuse of it is inevitable! Jesus' holy anger kindled against the ghastly, reckless traders had in essence signaled God's strongest message of disapproval to any human act of the desecrating of their body originally meant as residence of the Holy Spirit, in hedonistic tendencies.

Read these words of Prophet Jeremiah:

'Will ye steal, murder, and commit adultery, and swear falsely, and burn incense to Baal, and walk after other gods whom ye know not;

And come and stand before me in this house, which shall be called by my name …

Is this house, which is called by my name, become a den of robbers in your eyes?'
| Jeremiah 7:9 –11

Here are five 'home-run' hits:

- *Would you this very day recognize God is intrinsically concerned with what you do with 'your' very body He lent you?*

- *Would you reckon that prayerlessness is essentially an hedonistic act that denies God access to manifest through your vessel on earth?*

- *Did you ever conceive of prayerlessness as such as I've just described to you?*

- *(What other acts of sacrilege or desecration against God's living temple — which you are — could you think of right now?)*

- *Are you an hedonistic person?*

c.) *His compassion for the societal outcasts:*
Jesus categorically made clear the summary of His ministry in a public mission statement recorded by Dr. Luke:

'They that are whole need not a physician; but they that are sick. I came not to call the righteous, but sinners to repentance.'
| Luke 5:31–32

The money-changers and dove-sellers had not been

hungry for righteousness. Their hunger had been for money. They hadn't thirsted for the fulfilment of Christ's Kingdom; they hadn't recognized the very presence of the Lord of the Kingdom at the Temple while He had been there. Funny isn't it that some other group of people had!

Guess who they had been?

The destitute; those rejected by the society, the sick, the helpless, the blind and the lame had yielded their hearts unto Him. The scripture says:

'And the blind and the lame came to him in the temple; and he healed them'
 | Matthew 21:14.

They came to Jesus!

How could the blind who had perfect limbs yet no sight have led the lame who had a 20-20 vision but no limb-movements, except they had inter-depended on each other? Think about it: They must have had an agreement to mutually exchange each party's inability for ability. I believe the blind had carried the lame while the lame had shouted directions to his comrade in order to get to Jesus. Bottom-line? They all had 'rolled', at Jesus' feet! Here we see in action, the principle of deference — and not differentiation. Completeness; not competition! Often times than never, life's troubles could really make a community of lovers achieve farther much more than a communion of haters!

Jesus had demonstrated His willingness both to heal and make whole any who comes to Him! The profiteering folks had had their souls blighted by mammon — the demon of the love of money. Positions have so quickly swiveled round: The societal outcasts had become Kingdom-heirs!

- *Ask yourself: 'Is my heart overtaken by surfeiting?'*

d.) His demonstration of authority over the demonic operating through inanimate living beings: No Hebrew of Jesus' day knew the real meaning of 'Bethany': It was not a Hebrew name. 'Beth' however means 'a house' or 'a compound'. The word 'Beth-ania' is of Chaldean origin — and had meant the 'region of dates'. In other words, date plants were the predominant harvests from this region of a village close to Jerusalem!

So, what had a lone, solitary fig-tree been doing on a plantation of dates? In horticulture — that branch of agriculture that primarily deals with garden-cultivation and management; this lone fig amidst a plantation of dates would be regarded as a weed! Period!

Do you remember what Jesus had earlier taught about weeds in Matthew's gospel?

The Son of God had affirmed His Heavenly Father as the Husbandman in John 15:1. Says He:

'I AM the true vine, and my Father is the husbandman.'

We know a 'Husbandman' is a synonym for a 'Gardener'. The Vinedresser. The Horti-culturist. Jesus says: 'Every plant, which my heavenly Father hath not planted, shall be rooted up.'
| Matthew 15:13

Firstly, that fig tree in the Bethany village had been an illegitimate tree. Its destiny had been foretold, as is the destiny of every strange planting in your physical body!

Secondly, that illegitimate fig tree it had been which had first called for undue attention with its huge green foliage when it had not been its fruiting season! That had been its guise to mask reality in deception; for figs only had plenty foliage when they had borne succulent fruits!

Thirdly, the illegitimate, deceptive fig tree had first struck conversation with Jesus Chris, albeit in the spiritual! Did you notice that? Saint Mark the Roman had! He had been the most sensitive of the synoptic writers to have picked up the conversation in the spirit. He had written:

'And Jesus answered and said unto it …'
| Mark 11:14

No one obviously answers anybody except someone first struck a conversation with them. That's just the way it is! Now, let's recount the events from both Matthew's and Mark's perspectives:

'Now in the morning as he returned into the city, he hungered.

And when he saw a fig tree in the way, he came to it, and found nothing thereon, but leaves only, and said unto it,

Let no fruit grow on thee henceforward for ever. And presently the fig tree withered away.'

| Matthew 21:18-20

'And in the morning, as they passed by, they saw the fig tree dried up from the roots.

And Peter calling to remembrance, saith unto him, Master, behold, the fig tree which thou cursedst is withered away.

And Jesus answering saith unto them, Have faith in God.

For verily I say unto you that whosoever shall say unto this mountain be thou removed, and be thou cast into the sea; and shalt not doubt in his heart, but shall believe that those things which he saith shall come to pass; he shall have whatsoever he saith.'

| Mark 11:20-23

The conclusion Mark had drawn had remained exactly the same as Matthew 15:13 captioned in my notes as: 'Rooted Up!'

Hence, Jesus the Son of the living God undoubtedly had mandated it ever will remain His Father's perfect will for His children to enforce their authority to uproot any illegitimate spiritual operation that could be operative in the lives of humans! Wherever the enemy lurks, as soon we gained word of it, we must take authority in the name of Jesus; rebuke the devil through the words of our mouth — and expect him and his cohorts to flee!

- *Are you an authoritative child of God?*

e.) His avoidance of distractions:
As Jesus had been about His business in the Temple on Day 2 of His arrival in Jerusalem, He had taught the people whom He had likened to 'sheep without a shepherd'. They had soaked in all of His teachings until the chief priests and elders had shown up at his lecture. They had just one thing in mind: Challenge His authority! Of course, their mindsets had been diabolic.

'And when he was come into the temple, the chief priests and the elders of the people came to him as he was teaching, and said, By what authority does thou these things? And who gave thee this authority?

And Jesus answered and said unto them, I also will ask you one thing, which if ye tell me, I in likewise will tell you by what authority I do these things.

The baptism of John, whence was it? From heaven, or of men? And they reasoned with themselves, saying, If we shall say, From heaven; he will say unto us, Why did ye not believe him?

But if we shall say, of men; we fear the people; for all hold John as a prophet.

And they answered Jesus, and said, We cannot tell. And he said unto them, Neither tell I you by what authority I do these things.'
| Matthew 21:23-27

The devil will always attempt to undercut your calling and anointing through distractions and challenges. We, like Jesus cannot afford to be distracted from the vision of Zion either by insolent and ridiculous or outright confrontation! That is why we must fulfil every law of the land to operate according to set precepts and statutory decrees of the law that govern our religious freedom charter!

- *Is your ministry abiding by the set groundrules of your country of operation?*

f.) His bringing to the fore, the definition of Jewish impenitence and rejection of His message, Jesus had proceeded to tell His disciples, two parables.

Here's the first:

I.
'But what think ye? A certain man had two sons; and he came to the first, and said, Son, go work today in my vineyard.

He answered and said, I will not: But afterward he repented, and went.

And he came to the second, and said likewise. And he answered and said, I go, sir; and went not.

Whether of them twain did the will of his father?

They say unto him, The first. Jesus saith unto them, Verily I say unto you, That the publicans and the harlots go into the kingdom of God before you.'

| Matthew 21:28-31

Two lessons the Master had aimed to deliver through His teaching this parable:

i.) He had inarguably visibly demonstrated the issue of their hearts' impenitence and slyness, coupled with outright denial by contrasting it with a penitent heart that leads to a re-consideration to heed the Father's bidding! An un-equaled perfect obedience is the Father's expectation of us. Sometimes; however, we just don't seem to get it. Possibly our moods and emotions are wedges in the door to our obedience of Him! It's very interesting Jesus had made mention of the prostitutes proceeding into Heaven farther ahead of the proud, big-headed theological lecturers. They had shot themselves in the heads via their callous hearts!

Even in His last few days on earth, Jesus had modeled that it's far better to be late — than never, in obeying the Father! A changed mindset — for that's what true repentance is — can indeed avail much for the Lord! It exhibits both an after-thought and an after-care attitude to the Father's bidding.

ii.) *His teaching of this parable had been intended both to correct and encourage the faithful laborer in God's vineyard who now had grown disgruntled and disenchanted with the Husbandman.*

This particular dude had arrived earliest for the day's job description at 5 a.m. But towards the end of the shift however, he had grown critical of the Husbandman's integrity simply because He had also equally hired more hands at 9 a.m., 12 noon,

3 p.m. and 5 p.m., for just the same penny-a-day wage.

When the wages had been paid, every laborer had received exact same contracted amount of a penny — and our friend had grown furious. He had felt cheated, maligned and discouraged. He had questioned the morale of the husbandman! This interesting story is found in Matthew 20:1-16.

Now, whether a co-worker commenced labor at mid-day or close to the end of the shift should never cause us to treat with pickle, the seeming lackluster of their character. That pre-occupation clearly isn't your prerogative! If any laborer in the Lord's vineyard be late in reporting for the call, our greatest joy it ought to be to support such; not castigate them. We ought rather to rejoice that both they and we would indeed have our rewards for our protracted months and years of labor with patience!

II.
The second parable Jesus Christ had counted worthy of mention to the hearing of the antagonistic religious leaders — and akin to our subject of discussion — is found in Matthew 21:33 until the end.

In this riveting teaching about a Vineyard owner, the husbandmen (caretakers), His servants and son, we undeniably witness the hardened hearts of the husbandmen to offer to the Husbandman, yields from off His land. He had sent servants — that is, the old time prophets to demand yield — but they had been mistreated and eventually killed by the Jewry. Finally, He had sent His Son, His only Heir whom also they had arrested, tortured and executed!

Unfortunately for any remnant of today's scribes and elders, God has a potent remnant of saints scattered across the face of the earth who wield tremendous power with Him. These will not allow the demonic-infested minds of religious bigots like yourselves, a slight chance to seize upon His remnants!

- *Ask yourself: 'Am I a religious bigot?'*

g.) His correction of an erroneous view on evangelism (Matthew 22:1–14):
Having warned of the consequences of the continual hardening of the hearts of the Jewry towards God's plan of salvation until the completion of the Gentiles' grafting be accomplished, the Master had delivered a paradigm shift on His disciples'

erroneous concept of evangelism through the parable of the marriage feast.

Jesus had anchored His teaching on the template, saying: 'The wedding is ready but they which were bidden were not worthy' | Matthew 22:8. *The king therefore commanded His servants to: 'Go ye therefore into the highways, and as many as ye shall find, bid to the marriage. So, those servants went out into the highways, gathered together all as many as they found, both bad and good: And the wedding was furnished with guests'* | Matthew 22:9-10.

As I travel preaching the Gospel, I have met anointed ministers of the Gospel who have lamented of the hardness of hearts in their lands, thus encroaching their ministries' strengths on mere reserve-tank fuel capacities. In other words, they tether on toiling; there are no apparent results commensurate to their strangulating efforts over the years! To such, Jesus had delivered a change of strategy in evangelism. He seemed to have counseled a diversion of focus away from ungrateful souls who trifle their spirited efforts at saving and having the Gospel message preached to them! Gone were the days of mis-information when missioners on the mission fields had had to lay down their lives loving the mocking, unrepentant, hardened religious nuts who had plotted their demise! Jesus wisely counseled: 'Divert your focus onto receptive hearts!'

In a corresponding parable of the fruitless fig tree in Luke 13:6-9, the husbandman had needed to hew that tree down because it had encumbered much space. In a determining twist of fate, the vinedresser had pled for its life in the fourth year: 'Lord, let it alone this year also, till I shall dig about it, and dung it. If after the three TLC years, it still refuses to bud, then it may be felled!'

h.) His other concerns:
Jesus' other concerns had included:

• putting to silence the ignorance of the Sadducees who were predominantly Epicureans and lovers of fleshly pleasures (Matthew 22:23–33); His emphasis on the 'Greatest Commandment of Love', (Matthew 22:34–40); His delivery of eight scathing woes on the Pharisaic establishment (Matthew 23) — and His prediction of the Signs of the End (Matthew 24 & 25).

By the end of His five-day blitz of attacks on the corporate Jewry Establishment, they had had

> *pretty much enough of Him and His piercing words. The Bible says:*
>
> *'Then assembled together the chief priests, and the scribes, and the elders of the people, unto the palace of the high priest, who was also called Caiaphas,*
>
> *And consulted that they might take Jesus by subtilty, and kill Him.'*
> | Matthew 26:3-4
>
> • *perpetuity ordinance of the Holy Communion the same night of His betrayal and arrest as recorded in Matthew 26:26-30'."*

It is *not* my place to begin to describe to you the rapt attention of those who had heard this message. My *homiletics* this day had been much more effective than my *hermeneutics*, I presume. This was *not* a sign of weakness; rather, I always loved to emulate Apostle Paul's dual-approach: Making the gospel message very easily understandable by *all* while maintaining *relevance* with his audience!

Everywhere the Lord had sent me, this had been my motto; my style of delivery:

> "And unto the Jews I became as a Jew that I might

gain the Jew …

To the weak became I as weak, that I might gain the weak: I am made all things to all men, that I might by all means save some.

And this I do for the gospel's sake, that I might be partaker thereof with you"
　　　　　　　　　　　　| 1 Corinthians 9:20, 22-23

At this Good Friday morning service, I had closed the meeting with these words:

"Seeing what the last words of the Lord Jesus Christ were — and the scenario surrounding Him, what are we supposed to do, as believers in Jesus? Even Jesus had us admonished:

'Now learn a parable of the fig tree; When his branch is yet tender, and putteth forth leaves, ye know that summer is nigh:

So likewise when ye shall see all these things, know that it is near, even at the doors.'
　　　　　　　　　　　　| Matthew 24:32-33

In other words, Jesus had said, REALIZE THE END IS NEAR — for you haven't got much time left. The stopwatch in the Father's hand is ticking away!

Not only are we to realize the end is near; we are to constantly WATCH:

'Watch therefore: For ye know not what hour your Lord doth come.

But know this, if the goodman of the house had known in what watch the thief would come, he would have watched, and would not have suffered his house to be broken up.'
| Matthew 24:42-43

Watchfulness comprises of: Readiness. Vigilance. Continuance. Our Master enjoins us to readily and vigilantly pursue our daily assignments with diligence and hope. Each day ought to be spent as if it were our very last on earth! Jesus assures that if we faithfully watch, no one shall be caught unawares by His appearing in the clouds of glory.

The Price of Betrayal

What is the price of Judas' betrayal, therefore? There had been only two great players in this act all along only one of whom actually knew the price tag attached to betrayal!

Jesus' heart had been heavy with sorrow as He'd washed His disciples' feet — and had treated them to His Last Supper. It had been a very intense emotional atmosphere! One of the twelve disciples had been slightly uncomfortable even as the Master had accurately revealed: 'Verily I say unto you that one of you shall betray me.'

They had asked in turns: 'Is it I, Lord?' They had each received a negative answer until badass Judas had pretentiously requested the Lord's approval as he'd dipped his hands in the dish. Jesus Christ had seized upon that very opportunity to reveal the culprit:

'He that dippeth his hands with me in the dish, the same shall betray Me. The Son of man goeth as it is written of Him: But woe to that man by whom the Son of man is betrayed. It had been good for that man if he had not been born.'

Judas had pretentiously petitioned Jesus to confirm his question too in the negative like He had other disciples'. But no; Christ had had a positive reply for this cousin-traitor: 'It is you!'

The gavel had fallen!

Judas had gotten pretty angry — and had begun to excuse himself away from the large Upper Room even as the servant King had requested him to expedite his sly, wicked plans. Scripture says: Satan had 'entered into Judas called Iscariot.'
| Luke 22:3-4; Amplified Version.

He ultimately had negotiated his pernicious way to the authorities, in the same Temple Jesus had cleansed and purged of rogues and traders, only five days earlier! It was here he and the rulers had negotiated the price of his betrayal of Jesus Christ at thirty pieces of silver coins!

Isn't that outrageous?

Look, the audacity to undo the work of righteousness ever always had undone the audacious! Judas, through his insatiable, incurable and uncontrollable lust for money — and what things money can purchase had opened up his heart to the devil to 'enter into'.

- *The core-question is: 'What price are you willing to pay for betrayal?' Judas' price-ceiling had been pegged at mere thirty silver coins!*

Any wife can sure tell the very moment the devil had entered into her husband. Any child could tell when their parent had become an alien — much as could the vulnerable, their captors! Judas had bidden Jesus' request: Headed straight into the cold night to hatch his dark secret with the authorities of the night 'in the absence of the multitude' | Luke 22:6. Thus, he had never had the blissful opportunity to hear most of these same words you are now reading! He had not heard Jesus' last words, lest he had repented of his plans — an act that could have threatened to derail Jesus' mapped out journey onto the Cross.

Judas Iscariot's conscience had been 'seared with a hot iron'; fully sold to the devil. He had missed out on his inheritance, eternally: A totally worthless price to have paid for his act of betrayal!

Because the authorities had never disclosed to the betrayer what their true intent for initiating Jesus' arrest had been (which had always been to kill Him); once Judas had witnessed Jesus' sentence to death, he had been overcome with great guilt and shame. He had returned to the Temple — and had refunded the leaders, the money! He had discovered his folly — but it had been too late. He had departed the Temple, empty; hung himself and died before his redemption could have been purchased!"

The Re-kindling of Fire

By the time I had unburdened this word of the Lord at Harrow, the Holy Spirit had burdened a few of my listeners: The daily attendance had steadily increased with each day of ministration — culminating in a swell on the Easter Sunday morning worship.

However at the Good Friday service after the sermon, the Lord had said to me *"I want to demonstrate my healing power in this place."* As we had worshipped the Lord, He had called out a few words of knowledge. A middle-aged man in particular had sat on the second row of the pews at the front, to my right. His face is ever-fresh in my memory. I had seen a vision of a phlebotomist inserting a syringe into his left arm — and injecting a solution into his blood vein. Then the Lord had announced:

> *"There's someone here scheduled for a blood check-up not too long from now. At the last medical appointment, the personnel had said your blood had been unclear, but I the Lord have just cleared the impurities from your blood. When you get the result of the next test, it would announce to you:*

'It's clear!'

I AM the Perfecter of your faith!"

Ash and Donna Colbert (not their real names) were not members of the Endurance Church Ministries; they actually had attended our meeting from the neighboring town of Chatham. Glory to God; Ash had scuttled out of his seat, come to the altar — and testified unashamedly:

> "Yes, yes, thank You Jesus; thank You Jesus. I could feel a stirring in my body already!"

What a wonderful Healer!

As it had happened for Ash, that day had turned into a double-whammy miracle-day! When I had glanced at him occasionally — during my delivery — I had noticed him grimace and twitch the muscles of his face, periodically! The Lord had led us in a series of healing-confessions and I had asked everyone to voice out loud, after me, some words of authoritative declarations. Thereafter, the Holy Spirit had asked me to ask everyone to kindly:

> *"Just lay your hand on your belly; and gently rub that belly in a flowing, circular motion! Declare*

life unto your navel …"

I had long ago learnt the wisdom behind this verse:

"Whatsoever he saith unto you; do it" | John 2:5.

No matter how ridiculous His mandate to me could have sounded or looked; *if* I had heard His instruction, I'd just go ahead and obey! It takes real faith — without yielding to the temptation to use the word 'guts' — to obey the most absurd requests of the Lord. But at the end, there had always been great gain!

Simply rubbing protruding bellies, you would think should have been quite an easy task to accomplish by a complete set of faces that had been total strangers to a foreign speaker, set apart from the host minister-couple! Everybody had commenced the group task. A few had actually started laughing! I wouldn't know whether their caressing hands on their own belly-buttons had tickled them, or it had been pure, sheer joy of the Holy Spirit! Whatever it had been, I'd even noticed from the corner of my eyes some wives who had helped tickle their husbands' one-pack mounds! Many things a minister notices from behind the pulpit, I tell you — and he / she just must let them pass. But *not* this brother. He'd sat there staring at me — and *not* rubbing his belly! Up until today, I never mustered the courage to inquire from him what had gone on in his mind! Immediately, the voice of the Lord had said to me:

"Get you down to him, quickly. Lay your hand on his belly — and rub your anointing in, on it!"

I had hopped down from that stage as fast as a bolt of lightning! I had complied with the Holy Spirit's instruction. I had gone straight to him and had started rubbing his belly while he'd continued to sit-stare at me! I hoped I hadn't transgressed. But I had totally, completely ignored him. Soon, I had noticed a conspicuous mass; a mass, the size of half an American football diametrically violating his belly space in a breach position!

"It's a tumor", the Holy Spirit had whispered in my inner ears. Wow!

Now, it had suddenly apparently become clear the reason for his grimaces while I had preached! Still cupping the tumor, I had spoken calmly addressing it: *"You tumor, let go. De-escalate. Puff down. Start to shrink, in Jesus name. You are healed. Hallelujah!"*

After the meeting, Ash and his wife had returned to the altar, publicly attesting the miraculous power of the All-knowing God. *"We had kept Ash's diagnosis away from friends and families — and look at what God has done here today,"* Donna had said. *"We thank God for your obedience to come here, Dr. Joseph."* She also had confirmed that Ash indeed had been scheduled for a blood test. That was a prerequisite routine for him to be able to meet with the medical consultant who had monitored the tumor!

As recently as a month before the completion of this book, my office had gotten in touch with the couple to hear of his healing-journey. Both Ash and Donna had indeed confirmed the goodness of the Lord: His blood had become normal as the Holy Spirit had said, and the tumor had turned out benign, having also shrunken very considerably. Today, Ash is alive; healthier and more active than in 2015 before he had encountered the healing power of God!

Concluding Windsor & Harrow Visits

Space and time wouldn't permit me to recount each substantial *fire* miracle we had witnessed in Harrow, Ontario, Canada. However, *PULSE Publishing House* had in 2016 summarily published an interesting, 65-paged mini-book: *'Your New Beginning'*. I would recommend it to you for a quick read. Here's an excerpt of one of the outstanding miracles that had been shared in it — reproduced with permission:

"Meanwhile, as we completed the conference April 6th, 2015 with a Ministerial Leadership Seminar, participant-ministers from various other denominations and ministries had gracefully interceded for the local churches and ministries in the region along with my family; followed by the Sammy Joseph Ministries, the vision — and I.

It was deeply a poignant time for me, personally speaking. I had come to Canada as a vessel of God's grace — and having being received as such had reciprocally warmed my heart. I had made new friends and forged deeper spiritual alliances. Now, it was time to depart. Sometimes, I encounter an inner pain at the conclusion of wonderful meetings such as this. Gratefully, I have a family to return to — and a ministry to do, back home until another mission opportunity beckons!

Meanwhile in Harrow, as the International Experience Harvestways Conference had concluded, Dr. Taylor had handed me the white envelope which I presumed had contained an honorarium. The Holy Spirit had informed me of its appropriate end. I never even proceeded to see its contents. I knew I'd clearly heard Him say: 'Designated towards the Conifer Tree Felling!'

Almost immediately, I'd repeated what I'd heard to both pastor-couple host. They had only further confirmed the accuracy of the voice of the sweet Holy Spirit: 'There were two conifers' they chorused, in awe; 'we cut down one – and trusted the Lord to find the right guy to cut the other!'

Well, the right guy had been me: The Holy Spirit had found me! How rejoice-full I had been!

Other friends and ministers had hugged — and exchanged complimentary cards with one another, myself included. The elderly Rev. & Mrs. Richard Davies had a firm grasp of my right hand; they shook it ever so warmly in turns. (We had even posed for a snapshot together). They had told me the advent and summary of their ministries spanning close to fifty years in four or five minutes. Eventually, the aged servant of God had grabbed my right hand, laid his left hand on my shoulder and prophesied upon me.

Afterwards, a dear woman of God Helena Clark (not her real name) had offered to take me out to lunch — in the company of an older minister designated to chauffeur me for the day: Minister Rick Brockwick, an ex-US Marines and brother-in-law to the Senior Pastor. He it was who had driven me in his family's red Caddy with the silver-shiny wheels. (Now, that was the smoothest drive I ever rode on in my forty-seven years of existence!) We were in the very friendly atmosphere of Windsor's Applebees' in no time.

Once justice had been meted to the meals, our benefactor had removed from her coat lapel, a miniature, beautiful golden cross. She had decorated the left lapel of my greyish-blue jacket and said: 'The Holy Spirit instructed me to decorate you with this cross-lapel since you fight the battles of the Lord of Hosts! Wear it anywhere He may send you!'

I'd fought back the tears!

Before I could have uttered a word, she had narrated how she had debated whether or not to attend that final morning's session. She had really wanted to, but had lacked the means to even get gas pumped into her car. So she had prayed to the Lord to miraculously meet that crucial need if it was His perfect will for her to be at the meeting. God had answered the prayer through a friend she had ran into as she'd pursued her business that morning; that friend had gently pressed some amount of money into her hands. It had been just *enough to have paid her due bills for that week, pumped gas – and gotten her to the church venue on time. She had deducted her tithe, paid our meals – and folded the rest in a crinkled white envelope. She had pressed that envelope into my right hand. I'd tried to back down accepting it – but she hadn't budged. 'This is the very remnant of the seed a friend had given me earlier today, man of God' she had said; 'spend this on refreshment while you changed flights on your way back to England.' It was while I'd arrived Newark, New Jersey, that I'd discovered it had totaled $13 USD (thirteen dollars) which had been receipted, once it had entered into our ministries' books! (And now, in a simple act of obedience to the voice of the Holy Spirit, I have ever worn that cross emblem on my different coats' lapels everywhere I've been).*

Finally at the conference in Harrow, there had been yet another lady of tremendous faith and obedience at the same closing meeting of April 6th. She had 'wanted to have a personal word' with me before we had advanced to the Applebees'. When I had granted her audience, these unmistakable words had poured out from her heart:

'Thank you Dr. Joseph, for your obedience to come to Harrow, to hold this conference! I'm a widow

— and since my husband's passing, my whole life had almost approached a standstill. There had been an idea the Lord had given me shortly before my husband's passing about addressing the problem of men's homelessness in Chatham and providing them with a shelter in a christian setting. I have been sitting on it for some years now.

However, today as you spoke, I heard the Lord ask me to ask Him to ignite in me a new passion and zeal for this vision.

Now, I am ready: I feel the power of the Lord on the inside of me — to do His will!'

Within the space of a month of intensely seeking the face of the Father, consultations had begun with the city's clergy, churches and ministries. Even Chatham city officials had had a waft of the air of this vision gently drift at their sensory nerves. Canadian Television — Windsor also had helped raise awareness of same, interviewing Ms. Shavers and some team members at The New Beginning Ministries — Point of Hope on the local news! An ember had been fanned to flame.

I am persuaded to believe beyond all reasonable doubt, 'this vision could only have been God!' "

Chapter Seven
Stoked

7
Stoked

The second lozenge box on this international mission *feedback form* had been successfully ticked, glory to God. God had enlarged my scope of ministry and essential connections. The news of the fire the Holy Spirit had lit at the international television station — and Harrow had spread to Southfield, Detroit, U.S.A. As I had counted my remaining days in Canada with joy, I had begun to look forward to what the Lord had in mind for the church in the Motown city.

Right in affluent Southfield, Detroit, Michigan, USA, the second eldest of five sons of the erstwhile renowned late Apostle (Dr.) Charles Miles had caught wind of the turning turbines in the spirit, too. Even though he had been pre-informed of my impending visits to both Canada and the USA, no word had returned to us until April 2, 2015. That was the night of my appearance on the *TCT-TV* network. The man of God had watched that live broadcast that night and hadn't been able to resist the Spirit of the One Who had spoken through me. He had reached out with a message captured on the answering machine:

> *"This is Apostle Dr. Miles. Could you please ask Dr. Joseph to prepare to join me on my radio show Tuesday and Wednesday mornings by 9.55 a.m.? We go live at exactly 10 a.m. — and he will be ministering for thirty minutes. Then, it would be our pleasure to have him minister for us at our midweek Wednesday service en route his flight back to England!"*

Very truly, by 9.55 *a.m.* the following day, Tuesday April 7, 2015; the phone had rang. Dr. Miles' secretary had requested I hold the line for a transfer to the First Lady Monica, the wife of Dr. Miles. She had been exactly as sweet as her youngest brother — my friend — had pre-informed me: Very soft-spoken and most gracious! After we had exchanged pleasantries, Lady Monica had passed me onto her husband.

Once pleasantries had been exchanged, it had been a

matter of straight-to-the business with Dr. Miles. He too had been asked to stand-by for connection with the *Radio WMKM-Detroit* operator to connect us, live!

Radio WMKM-Detroit is an AM — amplitude modulation — station. Over three million listeners in Michigan State alone and three other border states of Ohio, Indiana and Wisconsin will be reached by this broadcast. As soon as he had introduced me, Dr. Miles had passed the mantle unto me to, as they say, "take it from there!" The following was the exact story I had started with that morning of the broadcast:

> *"A four-year old son of an English apple-farmer had accosted his dad onto the farm someday. Pointing to some of the apples on the ground not too far from the bottom of the tree, he had told his father with twinkles in his blue eyes: 'Father, I can tell you which of those apples are rotten.' The surprised father with a puzzled look had challenged him to show him 'how' — as if he had been a novice!*
>
> *The little man had taken a few proud steps forward before he had picked just one sore apple. 'Yeah; this very one!' he'd said — and had had a bite, just to prove his point! His bite had split the apple in two halves. "This very one it is; father, it has a bad heart." He had shown his father, the worm in its*

very heart!

When God looks at you, what does He see: An apple with a great, big, healthy heart — or a rotten one with worms in it?"

I had spoken on the *'Recognition of a Godly Heart'* with *Matthew 12:33-37* as my text. The rule of the thumb for me had always been:

a.) Should the talk be an exhortation or a short, ten-minute sharing, turn —
- *textual*; that is, the employment of just a scriptural reference verse as anchor, from which the speaker could add few, other supportive scriptural references;

b.) Should the message be an half-hour message, go —
- *topical*; that is, the use of different topical texts in the Bible to build a sermon; say for example the popular parables, a short psalm — or from one of the books of history / stories that best illustrates a sermon.

c.) Should your message be a three-quarter-of-an-hour or a fifty-minute sermon, try —
- *tropical*; just like the dense, virgin forests with plenty undergrowth of the tropical rain forests are

cleared and loosened employing different heavy machineries before seeding can ever take place, an experienced speaker may embrace the expository preaching style to buttress his / her exhaustive sermons!

It's just as simple for me as explained — and the Lord has always honored my rationale in choosing which style I engage. It is just my style; I am by no means advocating an adaptation by another! I firmly believe every servant of the Lord should develop their very own ministration-style and originality!

Dr. Billy Graham for instance, had pitched his sermons against the backdrop of current world events of his day. Dressed in smart suits adorned with loud ties; his youth and gaiety graced by swanky melodramatics that were too hard to miss, he had held his listeners, spell-bound. Pastor Benny Hinn on the other hand always had focused on the spontaneity of worship of the person of the Holy Spirit. Brother Kenneth Copeland had employed the prophetic gifts endowed him, coupled with those penetrating looks from those eagle-eyes and a pointed, stretched-out index finger that had always driven home the point. You work what best suits — and *works* for you! I always loved crispy illustrations, examples and anecdotes undergirding my teaching and prophetic unctions!

On the live radio-cast, I had spoken for approximately twelve minutes in the first halve — and had hardly noticed it. My friend had eavesdropped in on the broadcast from the basement office of their home. I had been upstairs in the living room, left alone with God — and the telephone's mouth-piece!

I had listened in as the announcer had customized the advert segment of the show with a melodic tune that had beautifully drawn the curtains on the first half of today's show! Dr. Taylor had pounded on the stairs in fast, loud footsteps. He had beamed wide smiles from behind those ubiquitous rims of his glasses; his head poked through the door, eyes lit on raised eyebrows — both hands in upheld 'thumbs up' sign. He'd motioned he had wanted to just check up on me if I had needed anything. I had shooed him off — and he had ever so quickly retraced his footsteps back to his den, very gingerly! Such is the unspoken joy of true friendship.

As I had wanted to wander away in my thoughts, the unmistakable voice of Apostle Miles' had yet again engaged the airwaves welcoming anyone who had just tuned in. He had also requested them to invite a friend or a neighbor to listen to the remaining quarter-hour broadcast. He had introduced me again — and this time, as a Prophet. That had caught my ears because hardly had anyone ever done that before now, even though I am one. I had been so very intrigued and excited!

The second half had disappeared faster than the first. I had begun to prophesy and give specific words of knowledge and wisdom. I had even described to exact details a thirty-one year-old lady having troubles settling down to find *the* right man to love and marry:

> *"You've always been 'used' and dumped! You have always loved the dudes — but they've always been a step ahead of you in the game! Here's the solution to your issue: God says: 'Stop prioritizing men above Me,' saith the Lord!*
>
> *Prioritize Him first, and He will cause the right man to locate you!"*

You see, when you've received a word like that for someone, it would be easy to flow in the lava of God's fire, the rest of the way!

It had been easiest for the entity called time to speed by, unrestrained! It had been an anointed time feeding the Word to countless thousands — and being fed too, even as I had preached.

Once the second day of broadcast had been accomplished, I knew I had *needed* a break. Just a short one! Anytime I had traveled, our ministries had always emphasized a point of clarity to our hosts never to stress on taking me shopping; that would only end up stuffing and puffing my travel case, anyway. I had never approached, neither departed the United States or Canada on two trolley cases — except once when there had been present, more than six trunk-cases as a family entourage flying out from Chicago back to England in 2003. Those days, airlines had allowed just one case per passenger — plus a hand luggage piece and a laptop carrier! Possessing an extra case had always attracted a surcharge of about $140 USD per 'standard' trunk-weight! Anyway, I had never engaged in an unbridled shopping spree at any given time, anywhere in the world. Rather than 'shop until you drop', I'd rather often preferred sight-seeing — or visiting historical landmarks. So in Windsor, I had asked for the latter!

Our Lady of the Rosary Catholic Church building in Windsor with its infamy as the 'lighthouse' for Rum-Runners in the Days of Prohibition had been our first port of call. I hadn't the patience to tour the entire area that afternoon: I guess the very boredom I had tried to get away from had starred me straight in the eyes. I couldn't be bothered. I had had enough!

I had asked for a drive on what we call countryside in England. Minister Rick Brockmann had driven through a highway that had cut through wide expanse of fields of hay and tall, wild grass. I had asked for us to roll down the windows of the Cadillac, so I could smell the air. God had since my childhood days blessed me with good olfactory nerves that had always connected me with locations, people or objects; no matter how long I had last met or contacted them. So I had smelled the fresh Canadian spring air!

I had also spotted white, massive, giant, windmill blades gently rotating in their worship of God's clearest blue sky above. Those rotating blades had dotted the expanse of the fields for miles on end! That early afternoon, I had learnt that Canada packages some composite-sized hydroelectric powers harvested from these wide expanses of solitary tablelands of Ontario — along with some turbine power-forms for trade to her only neighbor across the largest natural frontier in the world! That trading had been on a steady increase in the past decades!

For almost half-an-hour majorly, the fields had whizzed past us until we had noticed a signpost welcoming us into Chatham-Kent.

Brother Brockmann happened to be a sports car enthusiast. So he volunteered to drive me to the showroom of the main *GMC* in Chatham. Immediately we had arrived the venue, like an overtly excited kid, I'd hopped out of the car: I'd never felt ever so curious! He had made mention of the manager as his old buddy. So I had stridden towards the first assistant I'd encountered — and asked for the store manager by name. The manager had strolled towards me as I'd bounced towards him.

"Can I hop into the sports car — and have its feel sir?" I'd asked! Quickening pace, my tour-guide had leveled up. *"Oh, by the way, this is Dr. Joseph from Birmingham, England."* It was a quick introduction of me to the big gun, sensing his stiff reaction. As soon as he'd heard the name "England", he'd mellowed! His demeanor suddenly had become friendly. He had instantaneously started asking about the Queen, the Royal family — and the Monarchy!

I have always noticed that Canadians, — particularly Commonwealth Canada — have great respect and admiration for the British monarchy. The Monarchy still rules the Commonwealth of Nations. I wasn't going to let that bond break in my trusted hands! So we'd talked about the Monarchy in the space of about three to five minutes. And then, the Premiership; the British Premiership! After our pep talk and sensing my hot enthusiasm, the impressed manager had requested of one of his sales assistants, to avail him the different keys to *all* the fancy sports-cars in that wide, expansive room. There had been four sleek, heavily-built powerful *toys* in that place that evening but *just* one had caught my fancy: the *Chevy Camaro* sports.

In England, the normal everyday roads have a speed limit capped at 30 miles per hour. Our roads are regulated by insomniac, eagle-eyed, speed cameras! They sort of put anyone in a hold, somehow. There's no moral justification for me, whatsoever, to appear 'holier-than-thou' in this regard of my behind-the-scenes romance with the laser-lights: Sometimes I had not only beaten the speed cameras, but even the slow-to-react red lights! Despite my rascality, all I'd ever punched had been a three-penalty-point and a monetary fine of — I think — £125 GBP over a decade ago. Apart from that, my driving record is *almost* impeccable. But a dashing, rushing thought had invaded my mind as I'd taken my seat behind the wheel of the *Camaro*: Push the pedal to the chassis! Thank God for the arresting voice of the Spirit: *"Don't even attempt to drive that car!"*

That was all I'd heard. My enthusiasm had died down within me as quickly as an *F-16* aborting a take-off! So in the parked position, I had calmly surveyed the mechanics of the neo-computerized wonder-car, like a kitten in a strange enclosure. The manager had hopped into the passenger seat and my ex-US Marines guy had stood by the sidelines. The gracious boss had intimated me with the specific capabilities of the wonder, bullet-car, verbally! Wholly verbatim, in a matter of minutes!

I had left that *GMC* showroom that evening with a sudden bucket-list in my mind having a single item in it! I had been tremendously fulfilled. My pulse had been raised. I had been stoked, just by viewing a *Chevy Camaro*.

We humans have different ways of relaxing and dispelling tensions away from our systems. The experiences of my journeys that afternoon had both enriched and renewed me. The big *Sears* store close by had been my final port of relaxation call in Canada. There, I had purchased some smart wears for each of my children — and some gift items too, for a handful of our ministries' partners!

By the time we had returned to Windsor later that evening, my mind had been refreshed. I was now ready to re-focus on my preparations for ministering at *International Gospel Deliverance Center Church*, Southfield, Michigan, USA, in lesser than twenty-four hours' time!

CHAPTER EIGHT

Never Say: *I Ain't Got Nothin'*

8
Never Say: I Ain't Got Nothin'

Fires spread when fanned by hot dry winds. So also does the Gospel, *if* shared by hot souls with dry, parched and famished hearts! I said 'if' because of all the different groups that exist in the world, the 'Born-Again Christians' and the 'Evangelicals' are the shiest clans to propagate their beliefs! With this thought at the back of my mind, I had been convinced of the clarity of the message the Lord had impressed upon my heart to deliver at *IGDCC* in Southfield: *Someone has got something within them that could radically transform their destiny, but they don't even realize it!*

It was a mid-week service. The Apostle (Dr.) Miles and First Lady Monica had roundly welcomed —

and introduced me ever so warmly. As soon as I had gracefully accepted the microphone, the Spirit of the Lord had caught ahold of my tongue and declared:

> *"I am going to show you very quickly how you will never ever be broke, stranded, sick, or afflicted again, one day of your life.*
>
> *If you take heed unto — and obey — 2 Chronicles 20:20 with me, we shall be in for a pretty awesome time with the Lord. Now, scripture recorded King Jehoshaphat addressing the inhabitants of Judah in the wilderness of Tekoa:*
>
> *'Believe in the Lord your God, so shall ye be established; believe his prophets, so shall ye prosper.'*
>
> *Indeed God commands us through the author of its oldest book; Job:*
>
> *'If they obey and serve him, they shall spend their days in prosperity and their years in pleasure. But if they obey not, they shall perish by the sword, and they shall die without knowledge.'*
> | Job 36:11-12
>
> *David is recorded to have testified:*

'Let them shout for joy, and be glad, that favor my righteous cause; yea, let them say continually, Let the LORD be magnified, which hath pleasure in the prosperity of his servant.'

| Psalms 35:27

I have never stood before God's people to minister anywhere in the world, except I had exhaustively sought the face of the Lord in study, prayers and preparations. So this evening, within the one-hour-time limit gracefully allotted me by the Apostle; I'd love you to listen with the ears of your spirit. More, be ready to heed the voice of God through my mouth, for He has sent me for your liberation from all shackles!

I have titled this sermon: **Never Say I Ain't Got Nothin'.**

In that story told us in 2 Kings 4, we encountered the distressed wife of an anointed man of God. She too had probably hailed from the lineage of priests. But this son of the prophet had suddenly passed on intestate. And broke!

It wouldn't have been a huge problem to work through had he died intestate but rich! The real issue had been the minister in question had died broke; indebted with no known securities. For this reason, the bailiffs had been summoned by the creditors, to attend his family home! His widow's pleas for clemency had fallen on hardened hearts — and deaf ears!

Read with me, please, the two introductory verses:

> *'Now there cried a certain woman of the wives of the sons of the prophets unto Elisha, saying, Thy servant my husband is dead: and thou knowest that thy servant did fear the LORD: And the creditor is come to take unto him my two sons to be bondmen.*
>
> *And Elisha said unto her: What shall I do for thee? Tell me, what hast thou in thine house? And she said, Thine handmaid hath not anything in the house, save a pot of oil.'*
>
> | 2 Kings 4:1–2

Did you notice her plain, honest response to the Prophet's question: 'What have you in your house?' Her response had sounded perfectly normal and natural. But you see, if you would annihilate the spirit responsible for lack, you must not allow yourself to be brought to the ordinary level of the norm; the status quo!

The norm, obviously, is governed by the laws of

the natural senses. (When I say 'you'; I refer to the original specie God created you to be; that is essentially, the real you: Your spirit).

To deal the spirit of lack, poverty and indebtedness a deathly blow therefore, is to revert you to the original you! That means your current thinking pattern would have to change. You would have to let go of the mundane, normal status quo and adopt the supernatural, super-normal thoughts of God. Your language too would have to change into the same super-normal, scriptural words of confession. Your outlook on life generally, would have to become very super-normal, too. So also your thought-patterns would have to be virtuously super-natural as said in Philippians 4:6-8. Only the supernatural governs the natural. Not vice-versa!

By the time I have finished teaching — and anybody asks you: 'What have you in your house?'; you shall never be caught replaying the same old mindset, saying: I ain't got nothin'!

Don't you ever let your mouth be caught un-guarded, declaring: I ain't got nothin'! Moses at the brinks of the Red Sea had been confronted with just the same question. He had the past 40 years walked with God ever so intimately. He had just emancipated over 2 million brow-beaten Hebrew slaves from Egypt. He had stared at the 'impossible' sea — as it had billowed on its banks. The formidable Pharaoh and his elite forces had been in a hot pursuit from behind — and had slowly encroached; ever shrinking the distance between them! The confused, panic-stricken Hebrews had railed, raved and ranted. But Moses, deep in soul anguish had cried unto God!

It is interesting to note in their dialog that God had asked why Moses had cried unto Him. In other words: 'Moses, you know my acts; why would you become so disillusioned? Advance!'

'Into the Red Sea?', Moses had asked!

'Yes; you heard me right: Advance!'

And just as Moses had tried to fact-check the voice he had heard; God had spoken to him yet again: 'But lift thou up thy rod, and stretch out thine hand over the sea, and divide it: And the children of Israel shall go on dry ground through the midst of the sea' | Exodus 14:16.

But wait! About a generation before this encounter

at the Red Sea, God had taught Moses about this same message I am preaching to you this day. His classroom had been found in an open field of a bush in the desolate wilderness of Midian. An angel of the Lord had appeared unto him in a flame in the burning bush. The bush had burnt — but had not been consumed! This had been the occasion marking Moses' calling!

God would then nurture him in a process of commissioning — even though he had not been consecrated!

There's a huge difference between being called of God — and being consecrated to God! The former totals hearing and recognizing the voice of God burdening you for a life-time assignment. That call is a personal attestation to God's apprehension of you in a sacred time spent alone with Him. God rarely calls collectively, in a group; rather, His call entails a One-on-one encounter even though He may call that single one out, from within a group, family or people-group!

At 'your' call, God gives you a charge that will never violate His written word. This charge becomes your life's mandate requiring your life's pursuit and total focus if it must be achieved!

Remember Jesus Christ the Lord said: 'Many are called, but few are chosen' | Matthew 22:14. This is the dividing line that separates children from sons: Consecration in the furnace of a deepening, faithful, holy, close walk with God. This is that sieve that severs the consecrated one from just one who had only received a call!

Some 'called ones' today may indeed not yet have been initiated into a deeper walk with God. In other words, they have not been cultured for consecration, for the process of consecration is expedited mainly through divine mentorship. It is only those who have passed through this crucible of 'No Return' that are indeed able to attest unto the dependability of God's divine nature, His miraculous provision and that development of spiritual strength to fulfil the charge! The Psalmist wrote:

'He made known his ways unto Moses, his acts unto the children of Israel'
| Psalms 103:7

Moses had been schooled in understanding beyond just knowing the rudiments. He had been steeply consecrated:

But we know that 'it is a faithful saying: For if we be dead with him, we shall also live with him:

If we suffer, we shall also reign with him: If we deny him, he also will deny us.'
| 2 Timothy 2:11-12

Some other 'called ones' have no revelation of God's ways, so they pave their own ways! They can't be comfortable with entrusting God with their all! They often seek to be powerfully connected with mere mortals in order to forge on religious showmanship and artisanship. A daily deeper walk with the Lord in total abandonment, selflessness and holiness where humanity is exchanged for divinity is alien to them; they have short-changed themselves!

Unsheathing God's intimate layers however, ultimately leads anyone called by Him unto a consecrated lifestyle. God is both the Caller — and the Perfecter of all that are called by Him. They all travel one major highway of holiness and faith! It had taken Moses, the servant of God forty years to have been modeled into the exact stature of the leader God had had in mind! That shepherd's rod in his hands would hallmark his ministry. He had acquired the crooked rod in the wilderness of

Midian when he had changed occupation. After a display of sheer power of turning the rod into a serpent and back into same old crooked rod, God had instructed Moses:

'And thou shalt take this rod in thine hand, wherewith thou shalt do signs'
| Exodus 4:17.

In other words, 'Moses, you're now commissioned. You're now equipped'.

You see, there had never been any called of God whom He had failed to equip. That ill-regarded tool in your kitty has now become God's endowment! It's no more natural but supernatural. With it, you can never — and will never fail! This woman in our story — the wife of the late son of the prophet probably had this pot of oil in the house while her husband had gone borrowing. She had never realized what she had kept in her house!

Why Would an Anointed Person Go Bust?

i.) The very first reason any rascally son of the prophet should go bust is if they would not walk in consecration with the God Who had called them!

ii.) Second; any anointed son of the prophet would go indebted if they would not honor their spiritual parent; in this case, the Prophet Elisha. The anointing you honor is that same that rests upon and manifests in your life and ministry. Therefore, a tangible reason an anointed person goes bust is traceable to lack of honor!

iii.) Third reason spiritual people would stay broke is attributable to lack of financial acumen. This particular son of the prophet in question inarguably had lacked financial wisdom. A crucial part of his acquiring wisdom regarding successful financial stewardship includes taking heed to the teachings of his mentor on prosperity. This dude certainly had needed to have heeded how Prophet Elisha had honored God with his tithe and offerings; then first-fruits, seeds sown, vows and alms. No one ever had received supernatural increases when all they had done had been to moor down their financial rulings to the mere, physical, worldly economic realm, cued to fail!

iv.) Fourth; the Lord Jesus had mentioned the true-life story of the shrewd steward of the "certain rich man" in Luke 16 who had been too proud to dig. He had been quoted as saying 'I cannot dig' | Luke 16:3.

Laziness is a killer of destinies. Proverbs 12:24 assures us: 'The hand of the diligent shall bear rule: but the slothful shall be under tribute.' That steward had become a sloth. He had lost his job, yet had not dug. He had depended upon his artistry and smartness for a bailout. Even though it had worked for him in medieval times, today's state-of-the-art technology would have outwitted him. He would have been behind bars for deal-negotiations with investors behind the corporation's back!

Are you here today, caught up in a job-loss like this guy and just have not been bothered to search for a new job? Certainly, our friend hadn't bothered to train — or re-train and update his skills! This son of the prophet seems not to have bothered either, to advance himself — let alone anyone in his family! He had emerged a complete failure!

v.) The fifth reason a person may be born again and die indebted is due to laziness to renew their mind, daily.

You see the MGM Casino, Motor City Casino Hotel and Greek Town as we came into Detroit on the highway; those buildings up there with flashing red lights and the young beautiful pageant — wasting away? You see all the gambling wheels and spinning turntables? You see all those flashy cars and skimpy wears? You've probably even picked up the sweet-scent of the cigars?

Christian people possibly may be addicted to long-standing evil habits of gambling — and living life, fast 'n furious! Do you know why this is still possible? Because they have refused to renew their minds, daily! A child of God who had once been delivered from such lifestyles may once again revert to them like a dog returns to its vomit!

vi.) Sixth reason for being shackled by lack is greed: That is, biting more than you could chew! Possibly, this prophet had borrowed more money than he could afford to repay. Or he had borrowed without first researching and avoiding high street loan sharks.

vii.) Seventh; living with an undiagnosed mental illness — or in a denial of it; as well as coping with a prolonged state of undiagnosed, untreated depression would lead to poverty and penury.

viii.) Eighth; it seems he had not taught his wife the art of self-sustenance. He possibly could have encouraged her to solely depend on him, for money! That obviously would have been a major error —

particularly if he had been a low wage-earner!

Some men love to be in control of every facet of their spouse's life — even in the 'oikonomia' of the home. But nothing is less godly! In some countries and people-groups of the world, it is their culture to barricade the wife behind the doors of economic opportunities.

We must emerge a people of conviction, willing to critically examine before God's Spirit, what reason(s) keep us in financial bondage!

ix.) Ninth — and finally, any family would be plundered into economic chaos if the wife becomes un-cooperative with her husband in attaining financial prudence. Maybe this had been the kind of family this particular son of the prophet had maintained, I couldn't tell. All we know was she had had a 'pot of oil' under her roof — and had sat on it! She had never realized its monetary worth. She had never realized that just with the counsel of the prophet, that pot of oil would have translated her and her family from abject poverty and shame into a super-abundant prosperity!"

The Danger of Not Recognizing What's in Your Hands

"The Bible says through Prophet Hosea:

'My people are destroyed for lack of knowledge: because thou hast rejected knowledge, I will also reject thee, that thou shalt be no priest to me: seeing thou hast forgotten the law of thy God, I will also forget thy children.'

| Hosea 4:6

Do you see the fulfilment of every detail of this prophecy in the life of this particular son of the prophet, his wife and two sons?

Definitely!

Total extinction by waste, poverty and lack awaits anyone who dishonors the Word of God. If people will prefer to choose to remain unlearned about financial investments, shame and regrets become their inheritances! That care-free, anointed son of the prophet had self-purged himself and his clan from priesthood! I know because the bailiffs had seized upon his sons for bondmen! Their rascally father had died without knowledge. His posterity had well embarked on their way to the very par-

ched wasteland!

My quest for understanding your predicament today lies in your sincerest resolve to agree with me in questioning and answering yourself:

'What is in my hands?'

And I beg you to never reply: 'I ain't got nothin', Rev!'

Replying like that would tantamount to a wasted journey, time and expense for me, personally speaking! It would also be synonymous with the confirmation of the presence of a hardened heart, unable to decode the voice of Heaven at this very time!

But you probably cannot remain evasive to confronting your very self, any longer! Most often times than not, painful past experiences moor us onto a flag-post of penury. Some other times, our upbringing could trigger pain that spirals down ever so quickly to ruins. The abuse, hurts, rejection and emotional scars lie hidden and masked away by our epicurean lifestyles of mere, sheer pretense — and further pretense that leads to emptiness and bankruptcy! The sheer pain of abandonment engrained into Moses childhood or that suffered in the hands of the threatening Hebrew whistleblower in the Egyptian desert when he had stepped in to mediate and break a fight could have left him impoverished! He'd even had a first class experience of unpleasantness with the Pharaoh in his palace; but all that had further bolstered his resolve at following through with his consecrated vow: 'No Turning Back!' Following God's instruction, Moses had parted the Red Sea!

Joseph too had left nothing to chances. In fact, all his prestige had been stripped off of him. He had only one saving grace: Shackles! Those very shackles had further steeped his consecration to God. Instead of mooring his spirit, Joseph's prison-experience had instilled the rewarding disciplines of faithfulness and integrity in the consecrated ambassador of Heaven. Brother Joe had hearkened unto this same message amplified unto him by the same Spirit of God voicing through me to youward, today: 'Don't Say I Ain't Got Nothin'! The shackles hadn't deterred Joseph. Moses' abandonment and crime hadn't deterred him experiencing the fullness of the 'God of grace'. Your defective background ought not to hold you captive, either!

> *Joseph had purposed in the integrity of his heart: No Matter Where Both My Integrity and Faith in the Word Takes Me; I Would Gladly Serve Without Prejudice! Joseph had fashioned his shackles into instruments of his emancipation! I Psalms 105:17-22."*

By the time I had finished speaking these words, the Lord had begun confirming to me that chains of afflictions had begun to melt under His powerful anointing! There had been a middle-aged, African-American sister in the middle aisle-seat whom the Spirit of the Lord had just confirmed to me had had problems with her lungs for half a year; she had just instantly experienced God's healing power! The Spirit of the Lord had actually singled her out from the pulpit!

I had responded by vacating the pulpit pronto, before any could have pronounced "Jack Russell". Armed with a hand-held wireless microphone, I had demanded: *"Tell us what the Lord had just done for you, lady."* I'd put the mic. close to her mouth so everyone could hear from the horse's mouth:

> *"Well, prophet; I sat down here listening to you. Suddenly, I could feel a heatwave come all over me! You see, I have had this horrible bronchitis for 12 years; I had found it hard to breathe!*

The doctor had put me on a defibrillator to assist my breathing when I went to bed, nightly. The last six months have been a hell of a living: The machine had broken and I hadn't the money neither the insurance to order a new one. I hear the devil tell me, daily: 'I will snuff out your life soon.' I have been scared to death — and couldn't tell anyone.

Now I am grateful to God you were sent here of God: Now I am completely healed — and can breathe, again!"

The whole house had erupted in praise to our God!

I had further heightened the sister's faith by giving her lungs, a simple aerobic exercise: 'Breathe-in; hold-it — and breathe-out!' She obviously had gotten better with each inhale-exhale activity that had lasted about a minute in sequence. Thereafter, I had laid my right hand on her — and boom, to the floor she had sagged, slain by the power of the Holy Spirit!

There had been in attendance a Bishop and his wife whom the Lord had asked to 'Prepare to go start a new ministry in Birmingham, Alabama.' When I had given them the word of the Lord, it had been the exact confirmation of that which the Holy Spirit had spoken to them before their attendance of this meeting:

> *"The Lord wants you to go start a new ministry down south; in Alabama to be precise. Do not be afraid, I am gone ahead of you,' saith the Lord; 'I will make the crooked places straight — and surprise you when your obedience is complete. I will provide fountains of finances to flow in the desert!"*

This man of God had literally jumped for joy. It was only after his jubilation had occurred that his wife had looked at him, unbelievably — and reminded him that he couldn't bend his right knee since about half a year prior this very moment! His joints had been stiff. He had looked at his wife, very surprised, and then onto me. He had even exulted the more, the name of the Lord God, his Healer. The whole house had erupted in an uproar of adoration of our Jehovah Rapha — the African-American way, Detroit style!

After a while, the senior pastor had interrupted the service. He had had these very words to say:

> *"Look y'all; what you've been witnessing here tonight is the demonstration of the outpouring of the power and glory of God. We will not let this awesome prophet of God return to England with*

this kind of unction on him until he has prophesied upon everyone present here tonight!

Now, y'all file out as the ushers direct you and come to the prophet of God who will give you a word from heaven, anoint you with oil — and pray for you!"

You know as well as I do that you're about to be discovered and 'called out' if all you do as God's prophet is manufacture mere words of intelligence disguised as inspired prophetical messages! I personally think the prophet wouldn't have prophesied on any more than a maximum of ten people before he'd have been called out and shamed!

But I could sense the presence of the Lord, yet again, like as aforetime: I had become His amplifier. He would inspire divine *rhema* words into my spirit as they pertained to individuals and their situations. I had entered into another realm of divine flow.

I had gently prayed in my heavenly language, eyes closed before opening them to cast looks on faces; just as Jesus the Lord Himself had done when He had revealed the grievous sins in each of those callous men's hearts that had caught the woman in the act of adultery in *John 8:6-11*. Like His hands had written in the sand, my lips had parted to prophesy.

One David, the Apostle's armor-bearer had received a prophecy of divine provision. From yet another young lady, the Lord had cursed outright to the deepest roots, the spirit of rejection operating in her family lineage of preceding three generations. The Lord had identified that wicked spirit as been the cohort making doors slam shut in her face just as she had prepared to walk through them. As I had laid hands on her, she had fallen onto the floor, gently supported by a lady usher! Dr. Taylor had doubled as God's angel armor-bearer to me. He had worn the camera on his neck and had held in his hands, the cruise of oil from which I had scooped and anointed heads with!

God always sends prophets to declare in unmistakable words, His counsel unto His beloved people. The ministry of the prophets is not lesser needed today than the ministry of a pastor — or a tele-evangelist! I still wouldn't understand how a true prophet or teacher of God's word would allow anyone to cast aspersion on their calling. That ought not to be! God in His divine wisdom has His main, five-fold, ministry-gifts to the saints set in place, in no particular hierarchical order: The Apostles, Prophets, Evangelists, Pastors and Teachers:

- for the perfecting of the saints;
- for the work of the ministry — and,
- for the edification of the Body.

These ministries are indispensable, one to another; God gave them to His Body on earth for these essential functions:

> *"Till we come to the unity of the faith, and of the knowledge of the Son of God, unto a perfect measure of the stature of the fullness of Christ:*
>
> *But speaking the truth in love, may grow up into him in all things, which is the head, even Christ."*
> | Ephesians 4:13–14

Are We Under Fire?

Southfield, Detroit had been one graceful and anointed evening. By the time I had finished ministering, I had known I was only good enough for the mattress and pillow. I would be boarding a return flight to England, mid-day the following day. My host for the night, before taking me to their home had other quick plans however: *"I would love to drive you around Southfield to sight-see the most expensive suburb of Detroit,"* Dr. Miles had enthused! That exactly he had embarked upon doing for about a quarter of an hour, when suddenly, we had heard a loud 'pop' at approximately 10.23 p.m. I had literally 'jumped', despite being strapped tight onto my seat by the belt. (Remember the English never shared a common gun-culture with the Americans). With Detroit ranking top as the most violent city in gun crimes in the entire Unites States, I must have been justified in my adrenalin pump. Even the Apostle had asked me: *"Are we under fire?"* I had replied him: *"Apostle Prince, I should be the one asking you, sir!"*

Almost instinctively, the verdict of the disturbing sound had been passed by the immaculate Mercedes Sports' all-electric dash board. The car had registered an accurate reading of the pressure bar remaining in the affected driver's side, front tire. Within a couple of minutes of the dashboard's display, we had lost all reading. The car's small, oak-covered driving wheel had commenced shaking; the sturdy car, wobbling along on the dual-carriage highway on three remaining tires.

"Necessarily, we have to abandon our excursion," Apostle Miles had ruefully announced. *"But we gotta to keep dragging, man. We can't afford to stop on this highway: This is Detroit, Prophet Sammy!"*

I had whispered quick orders for God's angels to be on dispatch, my voice shaking, slightly!

No sooner had I prayed than the same side rear tire had gone 'pop'. At this, we surmised we had been under fire; not from human elements, but from the enemy of our souls! Oh, he had taken a serious beating in the service that night — and this had been all he could do to jeopardize our lives. Backlashes such as these *could* be anticipated after a huge victory over the devil. But you and I — *"as a sharp threshing instrument having teeth"* described by Prophet Isaiah — must guard against being caught unawares by Satan at such times. We cannot afford to be floored by reprisal attacks of the evil one! So we too had beefed up: The Apostle had kept dragging that sports car, anyway on two tires, wobbling and precariously tilted as it had been — even faster. Possibly at about 40 miles per hour, in my educated guess! I had begun to missile-launch in my heavenly language in rapid, spit-fire, assault volleys in the spirit realm!

"We just can't afford to stop — even if it means condemning both wheels and rhims; it's too dangerous to stop."

The dual carriage had been deserted for a few minutes now. We had been alone! Suddenly, a higher beam of light had lit the entire highway and had grown closer. It had been the church bus. The Holy Spirit had specifically instructed the driver to go look out for us. He'd come upon us charging down the highway at such unbelievable roar from two flat tires. When he had pulled up alongside us, he had started to yell across to his boss the testimony of how even though he had meant to go and drop off some church members along the opposite route, the Lord had specifically asked him to come fetch us. And there had been church in that van that night. Saints shouting, singing and praising the name of our All-knowing God! All of them in that white Ford van had given us a cloud-of-witness-covering, slowly driving behind us.

As our convoy had dragged on, the Apostle had pointed out: *"Look to your right Dr. Sammy; look at that mast on your right in the not-too-distant horizon, that's the world's largest African-American gospel network, right here in our Southfield."* It happened to have been the renowned Word Network television station headquarters. He had further informed me on their start and how God had helped them to become a world-wide broadcasting force to reckon with.

By the time he had pulled the tiny car into his driveway, we had expected total damage to the steering rack, two rhims and the brake-pads associated with both tires. The van-driver had gotten down ahead of us both, to assess the damage. What he had witnessed had blown his mind. He had started hitting his hands the hip-pop style and shouting: *"No man; no man, this ain't happening! For real? For real??"*

The Apostle had shifted his bulk from the low leather seats of the Merc. Sports. He too had clasped, clapped — and clapped again as he'd exuberantly praised God. I had simply stared in awe: There had not been a bend, a mark or a scratch on either rhims — or accessories. There had only been unbelievable shreds of tires hanging around the rhims. What we had witnessed at almost midnight that night had remained inexplicable to human logic. But we had — and still do have — a perfect understanding of the Holy One of Israel and His mighty angels. That had further fueled our mouths at His praise!

Epilog

Epilog

Obeying the Lord — and embarking on this mission was the most successful two-week outreach I ever had in my existence.

If reading this book has warmed your heart with Heaven's Spirit's fire — and you would love to accept Jesus Christ into your heart as Lord and Savior, pray with me thus:

"Dear Lord Jesus Christ,

I am sinner. Please forgive me of all ignorance, hurt and hatred I harbor toward You! I hereby do open the door of my heart unto You. Please come in. Forgive me my sins.

Cleanse — and save me! Write my name in the Book of Life. Thank you so very much!

Amen!"

If you prayed that prayer from your heart by faith, you've become a child of God. Write me today to: *reverendsammy@harvestways.org*

OR, write:

*Sammy Joseph Ministries
Box 15129, Birmingham, England,
United Kingdom, B45 5DJ*

I am waiting to read from you, today! Congratulations!

Similarly, if you'd love to invite me to minister — or help organize *International Experience Harvestways Conference* in your church, city or country, please write to the same address above.

Thank you, in Jesus' name!

Visit Us if You're in our City

The Harvestways Int'l Church
(Birmingham, U.K.)

Holloway Hall
Northfield, Birmingham,
England, United Kingdom
B31 1TT
Sundays: 12 noon
Wednesdays: 8pm
Home Cell Friday Prayer Meeting: 7pm
Tel: (+44) 7758195466 / 7854675159

e-mail: admin@harvestways.org

The Harvestways Int'l Church
(Nigeria)

1 Harvest Way, Off Elewura Street
Behind Zartech / GLO Office,
Off Elewura Street
Challenge, Ibadan, Oyo State,
Nigeria, West Africa.
Sundays: 9am & Tuesdays: 6pm
e-mail: nigeria@harvestways.org

Other Books by the Author

Other books by the author are available at any Christian bookshop near you, *Pulse Publishing House* locations or from our website: *harvestways.org*

Not A Mismatch
Affixing labels, numbers and digits on objects may not be inherently wrong, generally speaking; but when they have been employed for derogatory purposes, I may have to become the very first to confidently shoot my right hand up into the air, well above my head and demand logical explanations as to why that should be! My message to you therefore is very simple: your adverse life experiences or circumstances do not make you irrelevant. No matter your background, color, ethnicity or creed, the Creator has your very name written in the palms of His hands — and calls you by that name. You are not a misfit. You are not mismatched against your challenges; strength yet avails for your emancipation (168 pages)

Your New Beginning
A new beginning doesn't just show up. Success doesn't just arrive on anybody's laps; it only will arrive as a result of a deliberate, changed mindset. In this piece, the author makes the receptivity of the Word of God the catalyst to the change that births your desired new beginning. Says he: "Whenever or wherever occurs the reception of the words of the Lord into a human spirit, there is illumination … And not only illumination but warmth, glow, radiance, heat and the fire that purges! Thirsty for the Change; Hunger for the World!"

When the Chips Are DOWN

Based upon Jeremiah's observations in his elegiac poetic book of Lamentation, the author attempts to both depict the descriptions and manifested-traits of one whose chips are down! We may do well to arm our minds with a re-assurance of the possibility of experiencing at least a molting experience – just like the bald eagle – in our lifetime. Our individual reactions however, to adversity – and what we do with such rich experiences – are of great consequences that will impact the life we currently live and that futuristic life eternal!" You will be enraptured by the way the author has deployed sheer literary genus and a sharp, enrapturing writing style to describe the intuitive bald eagle – how he triumphs over his gruesome molting season in the wild. Learn in this book, your very personalized "way of escape" provided by the loving Heavenly Father out of the feelings of despair, despondency, desolation and depression. (110 pages)

APPRECIABLE Gifs

Seekers in quest of attaining inner peace with the heavenly Father, deepening satisfaction in their friendships/relationships, healings from life's brokenness – enhancing their sexuality and marriages need search no further. Within the pages of Appreciable Gifts lie your missing trophies! Irrespective of your status in life, if your heart desires to learn the most essential tips on how to 'spruce up' your 3-D relationships: vertical, ho-rizontal and downwards, 'Appreciable Gifts' will show you how! Read about: The Greatest Gift of All, The Gift of Restoration, The Gift of a True Friendship, The Gift of Sex & Sexuality in Committed Relationships, and; Cultivating the Gifts of Thanksgiving & Gratitude. Read and apply guideposts on the parameters of offering, accepting, cherishing, maintaining – and abounding in gifts! The messages therein will positively impact your relationships for a lifetime! (183 pages)

DESTROYING the Power of DELAY

This book is an expository piece of work, written in a scriptural, thought-provoking style. The author aimed at sharing with you from more than fifteen years of counseling in ministry, how to avoid the endearing long arms of delay; and if you're already entangled in a wild romance with the hated alien, the quickest way of escape from him. Furthermore, real-life issues such as 'Causes of Delay', 'Who Should Care for the Elderly?', 'Wisdom Handling Inextricable Covenant Relationships', 'Liberating Financial Management and Dealing with Indebtedness' are adequately discussed. Others topics include: 'How to Effectively Handle Mid-life Crisis, Depression, Barrenness' - etcetera! (220 pages)

GIDEON: Releasing the Potentials Within You

This book draws analogies from the life of Gideon (one of Israel's Judges) and applies them to how you can effectively release the hidden potentials within you. Written in easy, straightforward, simple language, you will find basic practical insights that will help lift you above common mediocrity levels in life! (176 pages)

Before You Step into Someone Else's Shoes

This book contains easy-to-do guides on how you will not repeat the costly mistakes made by others faced with a fresh opportunity to begin anew after suffering a heavy setback. We have also provided essential checklists to anyone willing to step into shoes ordained of God for them – as well as checkmating the mutineers! (46 pages)

Download *PULSE On-line*, freely at *www.harvestways.org*

Become a *Sammy Joseph Ministries* Vision Partner

Our commitment is to:

- Pray – and cover you daily in prayers, that God's undeniable blessings be upon your you and your household.
- Keep ministering the Word of God diligently.
- Minister to you once a month via a telephone call from us.
- Minister to you in a personal newsletter from Dr. Sammy Joseph – at least quarterly.
- Issue you an official partner certificate.
- Offer you from time to time, special, discounted gifts for your spiritual growth and upliftment through our website, programs and outreaches.

Your commitment is to:

- Pray for us always.
- Be committed to support our broadcasts, meetings and outreaches in your area.
- Support us financially with your monthly 'seed' as said in Philippians 4:17.
- Always speak positive words of affirmation on the ministry, Dr. Joseph – and his family.

If you would love:

- Host the *International Experience Harvestways Conference* in your country / region;
- Become a vision partner / supporter of *Sammy Joseph Ministries*; or
- Become a volunteer at any of our outreaches.

Please write:
*Sammy Joseph Ministries
P.O. Box 15129
Birmingham
West Midlands, England
B45 5DJ
admin@harvestways.org
Call: (+44) 7758195466 / 7854675159
Visit our website: www.harvestways.org*

THANK YOU!

Contact Addresses
In the United Kingdom & Europe
Pulse Publishing House
Sammy Joseph Ministries
Box 15129
Birmingham, England
West Midlands, U.K
B45 5DJ
Tel: *(+44) 7758195466 / 7854675159*
pulsepublishinghouse@harvestways.org

In Nigeria, West Africa
Pulse Publishing House
1 Harvest Way, Off Elewura Street
Behind Zartech / GLO Office,
Off Elewura Street
Challenge, Ibadan,
Nigeria, West Africa.
pulsepublishinghouse@harvestways.org

www.ingramcontent.com/pod-product-compliance
Lightning Source LLC
LaVergne TN
LVHW091253080426
835510LV00007B/247